A Field Guide

to the Study of American Literature

A Field Guide to the Study of American Literature

Harold H. Kolb, Jr.

University Press of Virginia
Charlottesville

THE UNIVERSITY PRESS OF VIRGINIA
Copyright © 1976 by the Rector and Visitors
of the University of Virginia

First published 1976

Library of Congress Cataloging in Publication Data

Kolb, Harold H., Jr.
  A field guide to the study of American literature.

  Includes indexes.
  1. American literature—Bibliography. I. Title. Z1225.K65   016.81
75-22033 ISBN 0-8139-0626-1 (cloth); ISBN 0-8139-0664-4 (paper)

Printed in the United States of America

Contents

Acknowledgments

This bibliography is an expansion of earlier mimeographed versions prepared for students at the University of Virginia, and I thank those students for their comments. I am also indebted to Courtney Goode, William Carr, and Harriet Pollack-Schloss for assistance; to Margaret Donato for expert typing; to colleagues Alan Howard, David Levin, Gary Lindberg, Raymond Nelson, Viola Hopkins Winner, and Charles Vandersee for suggestions; and to Kendon Stubbs, Reference Librarian at the University of Virginia Library, for sharing his encyclopedic knowledge.

INTRODUCTION

> Quels effroyables progrès nous avons accompli depuis
> lors! Les livres se sont multipliés d'une façon merveil-
> leuse au XVI⁰ siècle et au XVIII⁰. Aujourd'hui la pro-
> duction en est centuplée. Voici qu'on publie, seule-
> ment à Paris, cinquante volumes par jour, sans comp-
> ter les journaux. C'est une orgie monstrueuse. Nous en
> sortirons fous.
>
> Anatole France, *La vie littéraire*, 1888

The current expansion of scholarly activity and the bonanza
mining of new resources for literary study threaten to lead to a
despair over fertility similar to that engendered by the parent
explosion in population. In some respects it is even more
awesome. In the decade of the 1960s the population of the
United States increased by 11 percent; published scholarly
work during the period more than doubled. In the half century since the *PMLA Bibliography* was inaugurated in 1922, the
United States population has increased 91 percent; the
number of items appearing in the annual *Bibliography* has
increased 6600 percent. A representative index of expansion
can be compiled on virtually any author or topic from the
PMLA Bibliography (recently enlarged to four separate annual
volumes). Published items on Mark Twain, for example,
document the waxing tide:

1921-30	30 items
1931-40	67 items
1941-50	121 items
1951-60	350 items
1961-70	487 items

Swollen by expanded graduate programs, new fields of
inquiry, and automatic data processing, this tide shows no sign

of receding. An ever greater number of scholars is being produced. The first edition of James Woodress' *Dissertations in American Literature* listed some 2,500 titles for the sixty-five years from 1891 to 1955. The second edition contained 800 more dissertations for the next six years; the third edition showed 1,300 in the succeeding four-year period—an increase in the average per year from 39 to 133 to 260. The doctorate explosion in American literature is 2½ times greater than the population increase in India.

The fruits of this harvest are many and sweet, but its abundance is staggering for a scholar attempting to keep up even in narrowly defined specialties—and this at a time when humanists are feeling a greater need for breadth and interdisciplinary understanding. Some of the publication, especially in the bibliographical field, is duplicative and unnecessary, even irresponsible. It is hard to justify a need for *Drama Criticism* (1966), *A Guide to Critical Reviews* [of] *American Drama* (1966; 2nd ed. 1973), *Modern Drama: A Checklist of Critical Literature* (1967), *American Drama Criticism* (1967; supplement, 1970), *American Drama Bibliography* (1969), and *Dramatic Criticism Index* (1972). Since half of these volumes are issued by the same publisher, it is tempting to look for conspiracy as well as coincidence. The quality of scholarly criticism is also a topic of increasing concern. In his foreword to the most recent volume of *American Literary Scholarship,* editor J. A. Robbins spoke for many of his colleagues when he found it necessary to "turn to a topic of some sensitivity, with reluctance but with the belief that the point needs to be made. In the foreword to last year's *ALS* I noted the quantitative proliferation of scholarship. Some of this is genuine increment but, alas, some of it is detritus. In reading the eighteen chapter manuscripts for this year's volume, I was struck as never before by a reiterated refrain: this article adds nothing new, that one should never have been published."

The process of winnowing the bulk of current scholarship is both more crucial and more difficult than ever before, and the difficulties are multiplied for advanced undergraduate and graduate students because the increase in reference works and criticism has come at a time when introductory courses in research methods have been abolished and graduate programs have been streamlined and accelerated. The following selective bibliography of resources for the study of American literature is designed to assist the student who, faced with more miles to cover, is being asked to run them faster.

This bibliography is not merely another list; that is hardly needed. It is rather intended as an introduction to the most significant works currently available to the student of American literature, sufficiently annotated to indicate what they contain and how they are used. Many of the items, especially in Section I (Bibliographies), attempt to answer the question, Where should I begin? They are starting places for narrower and more specific paths of research. The user cannot find a biography of Richard Wright listed in this bibliography, but by using the index he can discover a source (Turner's *Afro-American Writers*) which lists such a volume. The section on literary history and criticism attempts to list the standard volumes to which scholars first turn and to which they return, as well as some recent books of interest. For the most part these works are thematically general (they exclude studies of individual authors) and specifically American (they exclude, for example, studies of the novel in favor of studies of the American novel, although there are a number of exceptions in the modern period). When possible and appropriate, the annotation attempts to capture the essential ideas of the work under discussion and the flavor of their presentation. A few works are included that exist on the outskirts of American literary study (such as Ahlstrom's *Religious History of the American People,* Dorson's *American Folklore,* Howard's *Our American Music,* Mencken's *American Language;* and several books dealing specifically with American Studies), but all are of importance to literary scholars. Sections IV and V (Editions and Series; Anthologies) have been designed with an eye to the graduate student who will soon be choosing texts for his own courses in American literature and recommending volumes for purchase by his school or college library. And an ancillary purpose of the whole is to provide a general introduction to the discipline and to the kinds of information—from how to obtain a free copy of *American Literary Scholarship* to the publications of the Center for Editions of American Authors— acquired by osmosis by scholars of American literature.

The items contained in this bibliography are drastically, if not desperately and at last even defiantly, selective. They are meant to serve as an introduction to key works, not as a complete or definitive or exhaustive listing. As is perhaps suggested by the notorious ennui of the sultans of the Turkish Empire—who in their heyday had fifteen hundred concubines—an excess of choice leads finally to enervation.

Key

Entries are arranged alphabetically within each section but numbered sequentially throughout the whole. Boldface cross-reference numbers refer to entries, not pages. The quotations used in annotations are drawn from the works under discussion. A "P" indicates that a paperbound edition was available according to the December 1974 edition of *Paperbound Books in Print*.

A Field Guide

to the Study of American Literature

I Bibliographies

Beginning students who are intimidated by the luxuriance even of this well-weeded garden might start with the following short list of basic bibliographical guides:

General bibliographies
  Nilon, *Bibliography of Bibliographies in American Literature* (**48**)
  Gohdes, *Bibliographical Guide to the Study of the Literature of the U.S.A.* (**25**)
  Jones, *Guide to American Literature and Its Background since 1890* (**35**)

Major authors
  Woodress, *Eight American Authors* (**66**)
  Rees and Harbert, *Fifteen American Authors before 1900* (**51**)
  Bryer, *Sixteen Modern American Authors* (**12**)
  Goldentree series
    Davis, *American Literature through Bryant; 1585-1830* (**18**)
    Clark, *American Literature: Poe through Garland* (**13**)
    Holman, *The American Novel through Henry James* (**32**)
    Nevius, *The American Novel: Sinclair Lewis to the Present* (**47**)
    Long, *American Drama from Its Beginnings to the Present* (**40**)
    Turner, *Afro-American Writers* (**62**)

Authors and subjects
  Spiller, *Literary History of the United States: Bibliography* (**58**)
  MLA International Bibliography (**45**)
  American Literary Scholarship (**5**)
  Leary, *Articles on American Literature* (**38**)

1.   Adelman, Irving. *Modern Drama: A Checklist of Critical Literature on Twentieth-Century Plays.* Metuchen, N.J.: Scarecrow Press, 1967.

A selective checklist of major criticism, including some play reviews, drawn from about 200 books and 350 periodicals. Coverage is of some 230 playwrights, both foreign and American, and is limited to the twentieth century. The book is arranged alphabetically by playwright, with each entry divided into sections of general commentary and criticism of specific plays. There is a bibliography of sources but no index. Cf. **9, 16, 49, 53, 55.**

2.   Adelman, Irving, and Rita Dworkin. *The Contemporary Novel: A Checklist of Critical Literature on the British and American Novel since 1945.* Metuchen, N.J.: Scarecrow Press, 1972.

   "We have attempted to survey, selectively, the critical literature on contemporary British and American novels. Generally, selections are from journals and books representing literary scholarship rather than from book reviews. There are exceptions, however, because of our own judgment of the unusual quality of a review. . . .

   "Novelists are included if they wrote after 1945 (such as Joseph Heller), if they wrote before 1945 but achieved their most significant recognition after 1945. . . . Once a writer qualified, all his or her work (before and after 1945) for which critiques could be found was included. . . . The cut-off date on material examined is 1968 for periodicals and 1969 for books."

   The volume is organized alphabetically by author (from Agee to Wright). Under each author, the entries—unannotated—are listed by individual novels and in categories labeled "General" and "Bibliography."

3.   Altick, Richard D., and Andrew Wright. *Selective Bibliography for the Study of English and American Literature.* 5th ed., rev. New York: Macmillan, 1975. P.

   A general bibliographical guide to literary studies, partially annotated. Includes "A Glossary of Useful Terms" and a brief introduction "On the Use of Scholarly Tools." Indexed.

4.   *American Literary Manuscripts: A Checklist of Holdings in Academic, Historical and Public Libraries in the United States.* Compiled and published under the auspices of the American Literature Group, Modern Language Association of America, by the Committee on Manuscript Holdings. Austin: University of Texas Press, 1960; rpt. 1971.

   A guide to "locating primary source materials relating to American authors" which lists, alphabetically by author, the number of manuscripts pertaining to approximately 2,350 authors held in 270 American libraries. A revised edition, which will add 400 new names, is planned for publication in 1976. See **29** and **46.**

5. *American Literary Scholarship: An Annual.* Ed. James Woodress (1965-69), J. Albert Robbins (1970—). Durham, N.C.: Duke University Press, 1965—.

    ALS consists of essays which are "critical as well as selectively bibliographical, combining the merits of both the scholarly article and essential bibliography." Each annual volume is organized so that half of the chapters "summarize the year's published work on individual authors" (Emerson, Thoreau, and Trancendentalism; Hawthorne; Melville; Whitman and Dickinson; Mark Twain; Henry James; Faulkner; Fitzgerald and Hemingway) and half "are devoted to genres and periods" (literature to 1800; nineteenth-century fiction; Poe and nineteenth-century poetry; fiction: 1900 to the 1930s; fiction: the 1930s to the present; poetry: 1900 to the 1930s; poetry: the 1930s to the present; drama; folklore; themes, topics, and criticism). A paperback edition of *ALS* is available (free of charge) only to members of the American Literature Section of the Modern Language Association (see **346**). The first volume covered the year 1963; publication generally occurs about eighteen months after the close of each calendar year. The series is indexed commencing with the 1964 volume (published 1966), which contains a retrospective index for the 1963 volume.

6. Blanck, Jacob. *Bibliography of American Literature.* New Haven: Yale University Press, 1955—.

    A selective bibliography which attempts to describe all first editions (books, pamphlets, broadsides, etc.) of approximately 300 authors whose works were, "for any reason, considered significant" from the Revolution to 1930. Thus Blanck's bibliography complements Evans' (**22**). Arranged alphabetically by author, each volume includes information on revisions, foreign editions, reprints, and "a selected list of bibliographical, biographical, and critical works concerning each author." Completed through Vol. VI (alphabetically from Henry Adams to Thomas William Parsons). Cf. **34.**

7. *Book Review Digest.* New York: H. W. Wilson Co., 1905—.

Issued monthly, with annual cumulative volumes, the *Digest* contains excerpts from reviews (from a selected list of seventy-five periodicals) of hardbound books published in the United States. It is arranged alphabetically by book author and includes a subject and title index. See next entry.

8. *Book Review Index.* Detroit: Gale Research Co., 1965-68, 1972—.

An annual which lists book reviews contained in 232 selected periodicals. See **7** and **33**.

9. Breed, Paul F. *Dramatic Criticism Index.* Detroit: Gale Research Co., 1972.

The most recent of this flourishing genre and perhaps the most comprehensive, the *Index* contains approximately 12,000 entries drawn from more than 630 books and over 200 periodicals. Just over 300 playwrights of all nationalities are represented, with each entry divided into sections of general commentary and criticism of individual plays. Coverage is primarily of the twentieth century, but major nineteenth-century writers are included if their works are still being performed. The book is arranged alphabetically by playwright and contains indexes of both titles and critics, with a bibliography of the books (but not the periodicals) used in research. Cf. **1, 16, 49, 53, 55**.

10. Brenni, Vito J. *American English: A Bibliography.* Philadelphia: University of Pennsylvania Press, 1964.

An annotated bibliography of 1,500 books and articles concerning the "English language spoken in the fifty states of the United States" which includes items published through 1961. There are sections on the history of American English; spelling; pronunciation; grammar, syntax, and usage; dialects; slang; loan words; and dictionaries. See **151, 225, 230, 238, 243**.

11. Bristol, Roger P. *Supplement to Charles Evans' American Bibliography.* Charlottesville: University Press of Virginia, 1970.

This supplement attempts to include all items printed in America before 1801 which were not listed in Evans' *American Bibliography* (**22**). It contains 11,262 entries, more than 7,000 of which are known to exist only in a single copy. "Following Evans' pattern, the entries are arranged alphabetically under each year from 1646 to 1800. Entries generally follow accepted practice for personal or corporate authors, with entry under title when the author is uncertain or pseudonymous."

Bristol has also published a separate *Index to Supplement to Charles Evans'* American Bibliography (Charlottesville: University Press of Virginia, 1971). Cf. **57**.

12. Bryer, Jackson R., ed. *Sixteen Modern American Authors: A Survey of Research and Criticism.* Durham, N.C.: Duke University Press, 1974. A revision of *Fifteen Modern American Authors,* published in 1969.

Modeled on *Eight American Authors* (**66**), this volume contains essays on Anderson, Cather, Hart Crane, Dreiser, Eliot, Faulkner, Fitzgerald, Frost, Hemingway, O'Neill, Pound, Robinson, Steinbeck, Stevens, W. C. Williams, and Wolfe. Each essay is divided into five major parts: bibliography, editions, manuscripts and letters, biography, and criticism. "The goal was as much breadth of coverage as was consistent with a good deal of depth. Thus, these essays are not designed as substitutes for scholarly bibliographies on the [sixteen] authors." Indexed.

13. Clark, Harry Hayden. *American Literature: Poe through Garland.* Goldentree Bibliographies in Language and Literature. New York: Appleton-Century-Crofts, 1971. P.

"Since the novel and the drama have been covered by others in the Goldentree series [see **32**, **40**, and **47**], the present bibliography, dealing with the authors whose work reached a peak between 1830 and 1914, will emphasize the writers' contribution to the short story, literary theory and criticism, social or travel commentary, history, and letters." Arranged alphabetically by author, works are listed under "Major American Writers" and "Lesser American Writers." "The entries under individual authors are generally arranged in the following sub-categories: Texts, Bibliographies, Biographies, Critical Studies." Also includes brief sections on bibliographies and reference works, backgrounds, and literary history.

14. Cline, Gloria S., and Jeffrey A. Baker. *An Index of British and American Poetry.* Metuchen, N.J.: Scarecrow Press, 1973.

A "reference source for criticisms of poems by British and American poets . . . from the earliest period to the twentieth century. . . . The books and periodicals indexed were selected primarily on the basis of their availability in college and university libraries." Since the emphasis is on interpretations published from 1960 to 1970, the *Index* serves as a useful supplement to Joseph Kuntz's *Poetry Explication* (**37**), which lists poetry explications printed during the period 1925-59.

15. Cohen, Hennig, ed. *Articles in American Studies, 1954-1968: A Cumulation of the Annual Bibliographies from* American Quarterly. 2 vols. Ann Arbor, Mich.: Pierian Press, 1972.

Includes three indexes: authors and main entries, personal names, and subject categories. See *AQ* (**333**).

16. Coleman, Arthur, and Gary R. Tyler. *Drama Criticism. Vol. I: A Checklist of Interpretation since 1940 of English and American Plays.* Denver: Alan Swallow, 1966.

"This Checklist is intended as a broad, nearly definitive, bibliography of all drama criticism—notable and obscure," appearing in periodicals and books from 1940 through 1964. Approximately 1,050 periodicals and 1,500 books were researched. "Entries appear in this listing only when they are of some interpretive value, or are of truly 'critical' nature." The checklist is divided into "Plays other than Shakespeare's" and "Plays of William Shakespeare." Includes three separate bibliographies: "a listing of books in which drama criticism was found"; a list of "books researched, but yielding no entries"; and "a partial list of those works printed between 1940 and 1964 which might contain drama criticism but which were not researched due to original publication prior to 1940." Cf. **1, 9, 49, 53, 55.**

17. Dargan, Marion. *Guide to American Biography, 1607-1933.* 2 vols. in 1. Albuquerque, N.M.: University of New Mexico Press, 1949-52.

Lists principal book-length and periodical biographies, with brief quotes from their reviews, as well as collective biographies, histories containing substantial biographical information, books on special aspects of the subject's life, and biographies of contemporaries. More than 750 figures have been selected on the bases of "achievement and historical importance," but there is some emphasis on "forgotten men." The books are arranged chronologically and divided into historical periods. Subject and name indexes are provided, as well as a checklist of sources. Cf. **231, 242.**

18. Davis, Richard Beale. *American Literature through Bryant, 1585-1830.* Goldentree Bibliographies in Language and Literature. New York: Appleton-Century-Crofts, 1969. P.

Divided into three sections: "The Colonial Period to 1763"; "The Revolutionary Period, 1763-1790"; "The Early National Period, 1791-1830." Each section includes alphabetically arranged bibliographies of American writers under the subheadings "Major Figures" and "Lesser Figures," as well as general categories of "Bibliography," "Anthologies," "Historical and Cultural Background," and "Literary History and Criticism." General introductory lists cover the entire period and include periodicals and newspapers as well as commentaries on them.

19. Dissertations. See the following discussion, the next item, and the entries for McNamee (**41**) and Woodress (**65**).

In general, there are two major bibliographies of United States doctoral dissertations: (*a*) a selective bibliography with abstracts and subject indexes, and (*b*) a comprehensive bibliography of all United States dissertations without abstracts or detailed subject indexing (until the 1973 publication of the *Comprehensive Dissertation Index*). The various titles of these two series are as follows:

a. The selective abstract bibliography (very selective until the mid-1950s, and it still omits some major institutions):
Microfilm Abstracts, 1938-51.
Dissertation Abstracts, 1952-69.
Dissertation Abstracts International, 1969—.

b. The comprehensive series (includes all institutions):
A List of American Doctoral Dissertations. Washington, D.C.: Library of Congress, 1912-38. Superseded by
Doctoral Dissertations Accepted by American Universities. New York: H. W. Wilson Co., 1933-54/55. This was superseded by *Index to American Doctoral Dissertations.* Ann Arbor, Mich.: University Microfilms, 1955/56-62/63. This was then retitled
American Doctoral Dissertations. 1963/64—.
Comprehensive Dissertation Index, 1861-1972. Ann Arbor, Mich.: Xerox University Microfilms, 1973. 37 vols. A new master list, indexed by both author and subject, of all American dissertations; some dissertations accepted by foreign universities are also included. Supplements covering all American doctoral dissertations accepted during the previous year will be published annually. The *Comprehensive Dissertation Index* is now the standard list of American dissertations, including those abstracted in *Dissertation Abstracts International.*

20. *Dissertation Abstracts International* (titled *Microfilm Abstracts,* 1938-51; *Dissertation Abstracts,* 1952-June 1969). Ann Arbor, Mich.: Xerox University Microfilms, 1938—.

A monthly compilation of abstracts of approximately 600 words, prepared by dissertation authors, arranged by subjects. For Vols. I-X of *Microfilm Abstracts* and Vols. XI-XXVI of *Dissertation Abstracts,* the inclusion and arrangement of title, author, or subject indexes vary. Beginning with Vol. XXVII (No. 1, July 1966), each volume of *DA* is divided into two parts: "Humanities" (A) and "Sciences" (B), which are bound separately. Cumulative subject and author indexes of both parts for the volume year are issued separately. "Beginning with Volume XXX, No. 1 [July 1969], *Dissertation Abstracts* changed its name to *Dissertation Abstracts International* to reflect the enlargement of University Microfilms' dissertation publication program by the addition of dissertations from European universities." Now 270 institutions are cooperating, although some major universities (e.g., Harvard and Chicago) are omitted. "*DAI* contains a mechanized Keyword Title Index by which the bibliographic entries are classified and arranged. This index lists the references alphabetically by 'Keywords' contained in the title. An Author Index is also available for each [monthly] issue of Sections (A) and (B)." Both indexes are cumulated annually.

21. Eichelberger, Clayton L. *A Guide to Critical Reviews of United States Fiction, 1870-1910.* 2 vols. Metuchen, N.J.: Scarecrow Press, 1971-74.

"This index is intended as a research tool designed to guide the student and scholar to representative contemporary critical comment [in thirty American, English, and Canadian periodicals] on fiction [some 5,500 titles] written by both major and minor United States writers and published during the 1870-1910 period. . . . [Since] a majority of the important critical reviews of books by authors who are conceded major rank are already known . . . the chief contribution of this guide is its listing of critical comment on minor titles and on works by minor authors."

The second volume "lists in a simplified bibliographic form roughly nine thousand additional contemporary critical notices [from an additional ten periodicals] of fiction produced by United States writers and published during the 1870-1910 period, thus expanding the original listing to over twenty thousand items. The guide is still far from comprehensive, however, and should, accordingly, be regarded as preliminary and tentative."

Eight American Authors, ed. Woodress (1971 ed.); Stovall (1956 ed.). See **66**.

22. Evans, Charles. *American Bibliography: A Chronological Dictionary of All Books, Pamphlets and Periodical Publications Printed in the U.S.. . . .1639-[1800]*. 14 vols. (Vol. XIII, completed by C. K. Shipton, covers to 1800. Vol. XIV is a cumulated author-title index compiled by Roger P. Bristol for the American Antiquarian Society.) Chicago and Worcester, Mass.: various publishers, 1903-59.

The detailed descriptions of works (which include author's name and dates, full publishing information, size and pagination, and location of copies) are arranged chronologically by year of publication and, under each year, alphabetically by author or first word of title when the author is unknown. Each volume includes an index of authors, a classified subject index, and a list of printers and publishers. The series describes a total of 39,162 items. See **11** for *Supplement,* **57** for *The Short-Title Evans.* Cf. **54**.

23. Gerstenberger, Donna, and George Hendrick. *The American Novel, 1789-1959: A Checklist of Twentieth-Century Criticism.* 2nd ed. Denver: Alan Swallow, 1969. P.

"The checklist is divided into two sections: criticism of individual authors and criticism of the American novel as a genre. In the first section we list criticism under three categories: (1) individual novels, (2) general studies, (3) bibliographies."

In 1970 Gerstenberger and Hendrick issued *A Checklist of Twentieth-Century Criticism on Novels Written since 1789.* Vol. II: *Criticism Written 1960-1968* (Chicago: Swallow Press), which covers material published 1960-68 and a few articles published before 1960 which were not included in the earlier volume.

24. Gerstenberger, Donna, and George Hendrick. *Third Directory of Periodicals Publishing Articles in English and American Literature and Language.* Chicago: Swallow Press, 1970. P.

Supersedes editions of 1960 and 1965. Brief descriptions of 547 periodicals which include title, editorial address, price, frequency of publication, year of founding, sponsor, and major fields of interest. Contains a subject index.

25. Gohdes, Clarence. *Bibliographical Guide to the Study of the Literature of the U.S.A.* 3rd ed. Durham, N.C.: Duke University Press, 1970.

"Undertakes to provide lists of books which will aid the professional student of the literature of the United States in the acquiring of information and in the techniques of research." Also lists "essential tools . . . for the study of American history, biography, art, religion, philosophy." Topically organized. Contains an appendix of biographical studies of 100 American authors, and separate indexes for subjects and authors.▼

26. Gohdes, Clarence. *Literature and Theater of the States and Regions of the U.S.A.: An Historical Bibliography.* Durham, N.C.: Duke University Press, 1967.

"Under the names of the 50 states, the dependencies and the principal regions, this volume lists monographs, anthologies, pamphlets, chapters of books, and periodical articles which will provide materials for the study of the local belles-lettres and theater of the U.S., from earliest times to the present. The literature and the theater are separately treated; the individual items are arranged alphabetically by author, editor, or compiler." Of special interest for local and regional studies.

27. Gross, Theodore L., and Stanley Wertheim. *Hawthorne, Melville, Stephen Crane: A Critical Bibliography.* New York: Free Press, 1971.

The section for each author contains subsections on chronology; editions, other primary materials, and bibliographies; biographies and critical biographies; and criticism, as well as a bibliographical index.

28. *A Guide to the Study of the United States of America: Representative Books Reflecting the Development of American Life and Thought.* Prepared under the direction of Roy P. Basler by Donald H. Mugridge and Blanche P. McCrum. Washington, D.C.: Library of Congress, 1960.

A topically arranged, annotated bibliography which includes chapters on literature and literary history and criticism. A supplement is in preparation.

29. Hamer, Philip M. *A Guide to Archives and Manuscripts in the United States.* New Haven: Yale University Press, 1961.

Contains "information about the archival [i.e., public records and documents] and manuscript holdings of some 1,300 depositories in the 50 States of the United States, the District of Columbia, Puerto Rico, and the Canal Zone. This information is organized in terms of entries for the individual depositories, and these entries are arranged alphabetically by States. . . . For each depository there is usually a general statement of its field of special interest and some indication of the size of its holdings." Includes a thorough index. Cf. **4** and **46.**

30. *Harvard Guide to American History.* Rev. ed. Ed. Frank Freidel et al. 2 vols. Cambridge, Mass.: Harvard University Press, 1974.

This standard guide to American historical scholarship has an ancestry that dates back to 1896 and has included, over the years, many distinguished historians as editors: Albert Bushnell Hart, Edward Channing, Frederick Jackson Turner, Oscar Handlin, Samuel Eliot Morison, Arthur M. Schlesinger (*père et fils*). Its purposes, set out in the first edition, have remained constant: "The immense mass of rich material on American history cannot be condensed into a single volume; and doubtless much has been omitted that ought to go in, or inserted that might well be left out. . . . However, the plan of the work does not admit of complete bibliographical information on any topic. It has been our endeavor to select out of the available material that likely to be most immediately useful to the searcher into political, social, constitutional, and economic history. For the antiquarian and the genealogist we have not been able to provide. We have, however, noted as many as possible of the more elaborate bibliographies, to serve as guides to more complete information."

The 1974 edition contains a "new arrangement of bibliographical materials . . . to make them more readily usable to present-day readers and scholars. A large part of the bibliography in Volume I appears under topical headings, and is heavily economic, social, and cultural. Volume I also contains the listing of biographies and personal accounts [and an introductory section on research methods and materials]. In Volume II the arrangement. . . is chronological, with an emphasis upon political and diplomatic history. . . . The terminal date of publication for books and articles is June 30, 1970."

31. Havlice, Patricia. *Index to American Author Bibliographies.* Metuchen, N.J.: Scarecrow Press, 1971.

"The purpose of this volume is to gather together under one cover as many American author bibliographies as possible which have been published in periodicals." There are 2,225 entries, arranged alphabetically, covering some 1,200 authors from colonial times to the present. Indexed.

32.   Holman, C. Hugh. *The American Novel through Henry James.* Goldentree Bibliographies in Language and Literature. New York: Appleton-Century-Crofts, 1966. P.

Alphabetically arranged selective lists of works under the general categories of bibliographies, reference works, American literary history, American publishing and bookselling, the novel as a form, histories of the American novel, special studies of the American novel. The remainder is divided into bibliographical lists for major and lesser American novelists. "The entries under individual novelists are generally arranged in the following sub-categories: Texts, Bibliography, Biographical and Critical Books, Critical Essays." Indexed. Cf. **47.**

33.   *An Index to Book Reviews in the Humanities.* Detroit: P. Thompson, 1960—.

An index to reviews appearing in a selected group of periodicals (averaging about 350). Issued quarterly, with an annual cumulation, and arranged alphabetically by author being reviewed. See **7** and **8.**

34.   Johnson, Merle. *American First Editions.* 1929. 4th ed., rev. and enl. Jacob Blanck, 1942; rpt. Cambridge, Mass.: Research Classics, 1962.

Intended largely as a guide for the rare book collector, but still useful for those authors not yet covered by Blanck (**6**), i.e., authors whose last names begin with P-Z.

35.   Jones, Howard Mumford, and Richard M. Ludwig. *Guide to American Literature and Its Backgrounds since 1890.* 4th ed., rev. and enl. Cambridge, Mass.: Harvard University Press, 1972. P.

"The first half of the guide provides background: a selected bibliography on relevant aspects of political, social, and intellectual history; a bibliography of scholarly and critical books on American literature; an annotated list of leading magazines relevant to literary production; and a chronological summary of American and world history from 1890 to 1971. The second half of the book is a guide to important original works, divided into two periods, 1890-1919 and 1920-1972. Its fifty-two reading lists, complete with introductory essays, are organized according to significant trends in the various genres."

36. Kaplan, Louis. *A Bibliography of American Autobiographies*. Madison: University of Wisconsin Press, 1961.

A "briefly annotated compilation of 6,377 autobiographies written by Americans from Colonial days through 1945." Indexed.

37. Kuntz, Joseph M. *Poetry Explication: A Checklist of Interpretation since 1925 of British and American Poems Past and Present*. Rev. ed. Denver: Alan Swallow, 1962. P.

An "index of poetry explications printed during the period 1925-1959," arranged alphabetically by poet. Lists main sources consulted. See **14** for criticism published 1960-70.

38. Leary, Lewis. *Articles on American Literature, 1900-1950*. Durham, N.C.: Duke University Press, 1954; rpt. 1970.

"An alphabetical listing of articles on American literature, primarily in English, appearing in periodicals from 1900 through 1950," which supersedes his *Articles on American Literature Appearing in Current Periodicals, 1920-1945*, published in 1947. The main portion of the book consists of lists of articles on individual American authors, arranged alphabetically. The remainder is divided into listings under topics and genres (e.g., Negro, humor, poetry).

In 1970 Leary brought his bibliography up to date with *Articles on American Literature, 1950-1967* (Durham, N.C.: Duke University Press). "That this volume is nearly twice the length of its predecessor is an indication of the burgeoning scholarship devoted to American literature in the last twenty years."

Literary History of the United States: Bibliography. See **58**.

39. *Literature and Society: A Selective Bibliography*. 3 vols.: *1950-55, 1956-60, 1961-65*. Ed. various hands for the General Topics VI Group of the Modern Language Association. Coral Gables, Fla.: University of Miami Press, 1956, 1962, 1967.

"In general, we have tried to focus upon three things: 1) the social provenance and status of the writers; 2) the social content of the literary works themselves; and 3) the problems of audience, together with the actual social influence of the writing. Thus, we may form some idea of the sociology of the writer, the influence of literature on society, and the social implications embodied in the corpus of literature. A study of the list will show how widely we have ranged in the fields of sociology, political science, economics, religion, and aesthetics, always bearing in mind that literature was our primary concern."

The bibliographies are divided into sections on books and articles appearing in periodicals, both annotated briefly. Indexed.

40. Long, E. Hudson. *American Drama from Its Beginnings to the Present.* Goldentree Bibliographies in Language and Literature. New York: Appleton-Century-Crofts, 1970. P.

Alphabetically arranged selective lists of criticism on major American dramatists and lesser American dramatists, emphasizing work published in the twentieth century. Preceding these lists are brief bibliographies of general reference works; American literary histories; bibliographies, anthologies, and histories of American drama; histories of the American theater; accounts of actors and producers; and studies of technique. There are also entries for special theatrical groups and special studies of the American drama. Includes an author index.

41. McNamee, Lawrence F. *Dissertations in English and American Literature: Theses Accepted by American, British and German Universities, 1865-1964.* New York: Bowker, 1968.

Dissertations (14,521 for the ninety-five-year period) are listed under "topical headings as general as 'American Literature' and as specialized as . . . 'Tobacco in Literature.'" The arrangement under each topic is chronological by date of dissertation completion. Entries include dissertation author, title, and university, and there is an index of major authors, a cross-index of authors (in which the major author discussed in a dissertation is cross-indexed with the author of the dissertation), and an alphabetic listing of authors of dissertations. American literature is treated as a subject on pages 713-858.

See also McNamee's *Dissertations in English and American Literature. Supplement One: Theses Accepted by American, British and German Universities, 1964-1968* (New York: Bowker, 1969). Lists 4,382 dissertations (including Canadian dissertations, which were omitted in the earlier work) for the five-year period. American literature is treated as a subject on pages 293-365. *Supplement Two,* covering the years 1969-73 and including British Commonwealth Universities, appeared in 1975. Cf. **19, 20, 65.**

42. Marshall, Thomas F. *An Analytical Index to* American Literature (*Volumes I-XXX, March 1929-January 1959*). Durham, N.C.: Duke University Press, 1963.

A thorough index to articles and book reviews which appeared in the journal *American Literature* (see **332**) during the dates listed. Indexed by authors, subjects, and authors of articles; separate book review index. An earlier edition covered Vols. I-XX.

43. Matthews, William. *American Diaries: An Annotated Bibliography of American Diaries Written prior to the Year 1861.* Berkeley: University of California Press, 1945. Rpt. Boston: J. S. Canner, 1959.

A year-by-year list, commencing with 1629, of published diaries written by Americans. Indexed.

In 1945 Matthews lamented that he had to omit the "innumerable manuscript diaries, published and unpublished, in the libraries of historical, genealogical, and antiquarian societies, in city and university libraries, and in private hands." He has now filled that gap with his recent *American Diaries in Manuscript: A Descriptive Bibliography, 1580-1954* (Athens: University of Georgia Press, 1974), which describes and lists the location of some 6,000 American manuscript diaries.

44. Modern Humanities Research Association. *Annual Bibliography of English Language and Literature, 1920—.* Cambridge, Eng., and London: various publishers, 1921—.

An annual (although some volumes cover two to three years) with various editors (British and American) which lists books (including references to book reviews), pamphlets, and periodical articles, including those by non-English and American scholars. The section on language is arranged by subject. The literature section is arranged by centuries with entries under genre and under authors' names. Indexed.

45. *MLA International Bibliography of Books and Articles on the Modern Languages and Literatures.*

Published annually by the Modern Language Association of America, the *MLA International Bibliography* is the best-known and most widely used bibliography in the field. A description of its development provides both a guide to the use of past issues and a history of burgeoning scholarship in the United States. The bibliography began in 1922 (with coverage for 1921) as a modest mention of some 600 items in a survey essay printed in the journal *Publications of the Modern Language Association (PMLA)*. This format, a continuation of the bibliographical essays that had been published in the *American Year Book* from 1910 to 1919, was preserved for five years. With the

"1926 Bibliography" (published 1927), a change was made to an unnumbered, partly annotated listing, which lasted for thirty years (1927-56). The 1956 issue introduced several changes: a new title ("Annual Bibliography"), numbered items, and a shift in focus from the work of American scholars only to that of scholars from all countries—a change which produced an immediate increase in size from 141 pages (1955) to 256 pages (1956). The "1958 Bibliography" added a new section for festschriften and other analyzed collections. In 1964 the present name was adopted. The next year, 1965 (coverage for 1964), saw the inauguration of the computerized author index. Mushrooming growth soon resulted in mitosis. The "1967 Bibliography" was divided into two sections—"Linguistics" and "Literature"; and two years later the *MLA International Bibliography* was detached from *PMLA* and published in four separate volumes: *General, English, American, Medieval and Neo-Latin, and Celtic Literatures (Folklore* added in 1970); *European, Asian, African, and Latin-American Literatures; Linguistics;* and *ACTFL Bibliography on Foreign Language Pedagogy.* The *1970 Bibliography* (published in 1971), seemingly the result of crossing a behemoth with an IBM 360 computer, indicates the course of the future. Produced entirely by electronic data processing (which will provide new storage and selective retrieval capabilities), it has 35 areas of coverage, scans nearly 2,500 journals and series, and contains 37,892 entries in the 823 pages of its four volumes—an increase of 6600 percent over the first bibliography in 1922. The rate of annual increase and the quantum jump produced by quadripartition in 1969 can be seen by comparing the *1970 Bibliography* with those for 1969 (36,461 entries; 723 pages) and 1968 (24,126 entries; 486 pages).

The *1970 MLA International Bibliography* is accompanied by a three-volume annual entitled *1970 MLA Abstracts* which is keyed by volume and item number to the first three volumes of the *Bibliography.* It "provides a classified collection of 1,744 two-hundred-word abstracts of journal articles on the modern languages and literatures to be used in conjunction with the annual *Bibliography*." The *1971 MLA Abstracts,* published in the spring of 1973, increases the coverage to 3,200 abstracts from 150 journals.

See entry for *PMLA* (**346**) and *MLA Style Sheet* (**239**); cf. Harrison T. Meserole, "The MLA Bibliographical System: Past, Present, and Future," *PMLA,* 86 (Sept. 1971), 580-86.

46. *National Union Catalog of Manuscript Collections.* Vol. I: Ann Arbor, Mich.: Edwards, 1962. Vols. II, III: Hamden, Conn.: Shoe String Press, 1964. Vol. IV—:Washington, D.C.: Library of Congress, 1965—.

The purpose of this series is to "achieve bibliographic control over the vast manuscript sources of American repositories" in much the same manner that such control has been achieved over published material in the principal Library of Congress and National Union catalogs. Toward this end, in 1958, the Library of Congress began soliciting reports from the nation's major repositories on the present state of their manuscript collections and began describing the contents of some 7,300 manuscript collections to be found in 400 of the responding repositories. At its last issue it had described over 31,000 collections and doubled the number of repositories covered. Eventually, full description of all collections in all recognized repositories is hoped for.

Individual descriptions are listed in catalog number order (thus making the indexes indispensable) with the name of the author (either individual or corporate) in bold type, followed by a descriptive title (e.g., "Papers 1740-1860"), location, a brief generic description of the contents, information on acquisition, and a note on research privileges or restrictions. Each volume is indexed separately and there are two-year (occasionally three-year) cumulative indexes. Cf. **4** and **29**.

47. Nevius, Blake. *The American Novel: Sinclair Lewis to the Present.* Goldentree Bibliographies in Language and Literature. New York: Appleton-Century-Crofts, 1970. P.

Contains alphabetically arranged bibliographies of criticism on forty-eight twentieth-century American novelists as well as a short section listing works on literary history, the novel as a form, and special studies of the American novel. Indexed. Cf. **32**.

48. Nilon, Charles H. *Bibliography of Bibliographies in American Literature.* New York: Bowker, 1970.

"The list may be used as a starting point by a person who wants bibliographical information on a particular author or subject in American literature." Includes some "books or essays that are bibliographical tools or studies" as well as bibliographies. Works are listed in four sections: bibliographies (includes "Basic American Bibliographies" and "General Bibliographies"), authors (arranged by century, seventeenth through twentieth), genres (literary history and criticism, drama, fiction, and poetry), and miscellaneous (thirty subheadings on such topics as almanacs, biographies, folklore, humor, Indian literature, music, religion, travels). Partially annotated. Indexed. Cf. **64**.

49. Palmer, Helen H., and Jane Anne Dyson. *American Drama Criticism: Interpretations, 1890-1965 Inclusive, of American Drama since the First Play Produced in America.* Hamden, Conn.: Shoe String Press, 1967.

Contains interpretations—often drawn from popular journals such as *Time, Life, Newsweek,* and *Catholic World*—published since 1890 of the plays of "all playwrights who have made a significant contribution to American theatre." A supplement, published in 1970, carries the bibliography through January 1967 and includes a few playwrights and publications not considered in the earlier volume. Cf. **1, 9, 16, 53, 55**.

50. Pownall, David E. *Articles on Twentieth Century Literature: An Annotated Bibliography, 1954 to 1970.* 7 vols. projected (4 vols. to date). New York: Kraus-Thomson, 1973—.

"Based on the journal *Twentieth Century Literature* [**351**], *Articles* is an expanded cumulation of the 12,000 entries [from the 'Current Bibliography' sections] which appeared in *Twentieth Century Literature* from 1955 through 1970. There are approximately 10,000 additional entries [from 300 other journals]. The bibliography is divided into two main categories—six volumes are devoted to authors as subjects and one volume to general literary subjects and an index to the authors of the articles . . . . The annotations either summarize the contents, state the article's conclusion, or indicate the nature of the article." The first three author volumes (George Abbe through Jaroslaw Iwaszkiewicz) appeared in May 1973. Volume IV (Jabès-Lytle) was issued in 1974.

51. Rees, Robert A., and Earl N. Harbert, eds. *Fifteen American Authors before 1900: Bibliographic Essays on Research and Criticism.* Madison: University of Wisconsin Press, 1971. P.

Following in the footsteps of *Eight American Authors* (**66**) and *Fifteen Modern American Authors* (**12**), each of seventeen essays "reviews the editions, biographies, and critical writings most significant in approaching the works of its subject of concern. Not detailed bibliographies, these essays evaluate the most significant research and criticism pertinent to their topics." Included are essays on Henry Adams, Bryant, Cooper,

Stephen Crane, Dickinson, Edwards, Franklin, Holmes, Howells, Irving, Longfellow, Lowell, Norris, Taylor, Whittier, literature of the Old South, and literature of the New South.

52. Rubin, Louis D., Jr. *A Bibliographical Guide to the Study of Southern Literature*. Baton Rouge: Louisiana State University Press,
1969. P.

Part I lists works on general topics (e.g., the Civil War,
Southwestern humorists). Part II consists of selective checklists
on 135 Southern writers. An appendix by J. A. Leo Lemay
extends the coverage to 68 additional writers of the colonial
South.

53. Ryan, Pat M. *American Drama Bibliography: A Checklist of Publications in English*. Fort Wayne: Fort Wayne Public Library, 1969.

The checklist "attempts to account for significant American
plays and playwrights from Colonial times to the present. No
attempt has been made to collect journalistic reviews of either
individual plays or historic performances; but a wide spectrum
of general critical writing—of varying quality—has been as-
sembled. English language books, articles and pamphlets . . .
are included, regardless of place or date of publication, and
notwithstanding the rarity of many items." Divided into sections on history and reference, general background, and individual authors. Cf. **1, 9, 16, 49, 55.**

54. Sabin, Joseph. *A Dictionary of Books Relating to America, from Its
Discovery to the Present Time* (also titled *Bibliotheca Americana*). 29
vols. Begun by Joseph Sabin, continued by Wilberforce Eames,
and completed by R. W. G. Vail for the Bibliographical Society
of America. New York, 1868-1936.

Sabin attempted to list all books and pamphlets, in any
language, "dealing with the political, governmental, military,
economic, social and religious history of the Western Hemisphere from the discovery of the New World until the date of
publication of the particular part of the *Dictionary* on which he
was at work." This was the general policy until Vol. XXI
(1929), when titles were restricted, for the most part, to works
published not later than 1876. For details of this and other
successive restrictions narrowing the scope of later volumes,
see the Introduction to Vol. XXIX. Approximately 100,000
titles are arranged alphabetically by author. Each entry includes location, collation, and a note on content, but there is no
index, a gap recently filled by John E. Molnar's three-volume
Author-Title Index to Joseph Sabin's Dictionary of Books Relating
to America (Metuchen, N.J.: Scarecrow Press, 1974). Cf. **22.**

55. Salem, James M. *A Guide to Critical Reviews.* Part I: *American Drama, 1909-1969.* 1966. 2nd ed., Metuchen, N.J.: Scarecrow Press, 1973.

The purpose is "to provide a bibliography of critical reviews of American plays on the New York stage from 1909 to 1969. . . . Some 290 dramatists are included in this volume, and over 1,700 plays. To the original 52 playwrights in the first edition I have added eighteenth, nineteenth, and twentieth century dramatists whose works appeared in New York during the past sixty years. I have entered American dramatists who are important in American dramatic history (Royall Tyler); who have written a play judged to be a critical success (David Rayfiel for *P.S. 193*); who have written a long running play (Anne Nichols for *Abie's Irish Rose,* 2,327 performances); who have written popular, commercial drama (Samuel Shipman's 23 plays); who have attempted to bring poetry to the theater (Robinson Jeffers); and promising new American playwrights (Leonard Melfi).

"The reviews cited in this volume are those which appeared in American or Canadian periodicals and in the *New York Times.* . . . No attempt has been made to include critical articles from the scholarly journals [which can be found in **1, 9, 16, 49, 53**]."

Other volumes of interest in this series include Part II, *The Musical,* and Part IV, *The Screenplay* (in 2 vols.).

56. Schatz, Walter. *The Directory of Afro-American Resources.* New York: Bowker, 1970.

"A documentation of the history of black America," this volume is modeled on the *National Union Catalog of Manuscript Collections* (**46**) and "consists chiefly of primary source materials and supporting documents" which are to be found in 5,365 collections on deposit in 2,108 institutions. In addition to governmental and public library sources, there is considerable emphasis on the holdings of state, local, and private agencies, as well as those of "organizations with civil rights programs and responsibilities, or with substantive interests in black America." Entries provide a description of each collection, its history and its content, as well as information about the repository and its research privileges. "The book is arranged geographically by state, then by city and by institutions within cities." It includes a selective, analytical index and a bibliography of secondary sources.

57. Shipton, Clifford K., and James E. Mooney. *National Index of American Imprints through 1800: The Short-Title Evans.* 2 vols. Worcester, Mass.: American Antiquarian Society and Barre Publishers, 1969; distributed by the University Press of Virginia, Charlottesville. The *National Index* grew out of the Early American Imprint Series (edited by the late Clifford Shipton when he was director of the American Antiquarian Society), a republication in microprint of the texts of some 49,000 books, pamphlets, and broadsides printed in America from 1639 through 1800.

"A short-title list of both Evans and additional items" arranged alphabetically by author. The *Short-Title* compilers attempt to correct Evans' errors, especially in regard to anonymity of authors. Entries include title, subject, place of publication, printer, date, and location of copy when known. This work is a useful addition to Evans' *American Bibliography* (**22**), but it does not include all of the items listed by Bristol in his *Supplement to Evans* (**11**).

58. Spiller, Robert E., et al. *Literary History of the United States: Bibliography.* 4th ed., rev. New York: Macmillan, 1974.

This essential work collects the bibliography originally published in 1948 as Vol. III of *Literary History of the United States* and the subsequent supplements of 1959 and 1972. "In 1963, the first 790 pages of this volume were combined with a bibliographical supplement of 268 pages that had been published as a separate volume in 1959. At that time, no attempt was made to repage the whole book or to remake the index. In 1972, a second bibliography supplement appeared, again as a separate volume of 366 pages. For this fourth edition, we have corrected errors in all three texts, combined the three tables of contents, repaged both supplements, and prepared an entirely new and enlarged index for the convenience of the users of this book. Thomas H. Johnson compiled and edited the original Bibliography, and Richard M. Ludwig the first and second Supplements." See also *Literary History of the United States: History* (**194**).

59. Stratman, Carl J. *American Theatrical Periodicals, 1798-1967: A Bibliographical Guide.* Durham, N.C.: Duke University Press, 1970.

Lists 685 periodicals (85 of which have not been located in any library) published in 122 cities and 31 states. The list is in chronological order based on date of first publication. It gives

names of editors, number of volumes, and libraries which hold
the periodicals (from a selected master list of 137 libraries).
The *Guide* is by no means comprehensive. It is, as Stratman
asserts, a "preliminary and tentative effort" and an invitation to
further research.

60. Tanselle, G. Thomas. *Guide to the Study of United States Imprints.*
2 vols. Cambridge, Mass.: Harvard University Press, 1971.
Following an introduction which traces the history of printing in America, the work is divided into nine sections: "bibliographies of imprints of particular localities; bibliographies of
works in particular genres; listings of all editions and printings
of works by individual writers; copyright records; catalogues of
auction houses, book dealers, exhibitions, institutional libraries, and private collections; retrospective book-trade direc-
tories; studies of individual printers and publishers; general
studies of printing and publishing; and checklists of secondary
material. The volume is designed to serve both as a guide to
research and as a practical manual for use in the process of
identifying, cataloguing, and recording printed matter."

61. Thurston, Jarvis, et al. *Short Fiction Criticism: A Checklist of
Interpretation since 1925 of Stories and Novelettes (American, British,
Continental), 1800-1958.* Denver: Alan Swallow, 1960. P.
Arranged by author, the work contains a list of sources
consulted, which includes both periodicals and books. The
books are listed either under "General" or under "Author
Checklists" if "the book treats no more than four authors, or is
devoted to a single author." See **63.**

62. Turner, Darwin T. *Afro-American Writers.* Goldentree Bibliographies in Language and Literature. New York: Appleton-
Century-Crofts, 1970. P.
"Although the focus is on literature and literary scholarship
of Afro-Americans, it has seemed advisable to include references to such related topics as the historical and sociological
backgrounds; art, music, journalism, and folklore; and critical
studies of uses of Africans and Afro-Americans as characters in
American literature." Divided into four parts: (1) "Aids to
Research" includes general bibliographies, collections, ency-
clopedias, reference works, periodicals; (2) "Backgrounds" includes autobiographies, essay collections, slave narratives, as
well as a wide variety of background references; (3)"Literary
History and Criticism" lists entries by genre; (4)"Afro-

American Writers" lists alphabetically works by each of the 135 authors included. Also included is a supplement listing some of the more significant recently published materials which were not included in the manuscript in time for initial publication. Indexed.

63. Walker, Warren S. *Twentieth-Century Short Story Explication: Interpretations, 1900-1966 Inclusive, of Short Fiction since 1800.* 2nd ed. Hamden, Conn.: Shoe String Press, 1967.

A bibliography of interpretative and explicatory articles appearing in books, monographs, and periodicals. Excludes source studies and biographical and background materials. Arranged by author. Indexed. Supplements I (1970) and II (1973) extend the coverage through 1972. See **61.**

64. Winchell, Constance M. *Guide to Reference Books.* 8th ed. Chicago: American Library Association, 1967. Supplements I-III, in paper, issued 1968-72.

This enlarged revision of Isadore Gilbert Mudge's *Guide* is the standard American guide to reference works. Essentially a bibliography of bibliographies, it organizes "reference books basic to research" in five categories: general reference works, the humanities, social sciences, history and area studies, and applied sciences. "Since a work of this kind cannot be all-inclusive, each section includes a selection of basic reference materials in that particular field. For additional titles and more specialized works, it will be necessary to consult the manuals, guides, and bibliographies devoted to subject fields." See **48.**

65. Woodress, James. *Dissertations in American Literature, 1891-1966.* Durham, N.C.: Duke University Press, 1968.

Revised and enlarged from earlier editions of 1957 and 1962. The titles are arranged by major authors and by general topics. Each entry includes dissertation author, title, date, and name of degree-granting institution. Contains an index of dissertation authors. See **19, 20, 41.**

66. Woodress, James, ed. *Eight American Authors: A Review of Research and Criticism.* Rev. ed. New York: Norton, 1971.

Eight American Authors originally appeared in 1956, edited by Floyd Stovall, in a format that has since been widely imitated. It consisted of substantial bibliographic essays which winnowed and evaluated the critical, biographical, and textual scholarship on Poe, Emerson, Hawthorne, Thoreau, Melville, Whitman, Mark Twain, and Henry James.

The revised edition covers scholarly works published through 1969. "The [original] essays by Jay B. Hubbell on Poe, Floyd Stovall on Emerson, Walter Blair on Hawthorne, Lewis Leary on Thoreau, and Harry H. Clark on Mark Twain have been greatly expanded. New essays are contributed by Roger Asselineau on Whitman, Nathalia Wright on Melville, and Robert Gale on Henry James." Unlike the original volume, the revised edition is indexed.

67.   Wright, Andrew. *A Reader's Guide to English and American Literature.* Glenview, Ill.: Scott, Foresman, 1970. P.

Claims to be a "key for those readers who want to be shown the way to the most reliable editions of the principal authors and the best works of biography and criticism." Pages 115-58 contain brief, largely unannotated lists of the editions, biography, and criticism for ninety-six American authors from Edward Taylor to Peter Taylor.

68.   Wright, Lyle H. *American Fiction: A Contribution toward a Bibliography.* 3 vols.: *American Fiction,1774-1850* (1948; 2nd ed., rev., 1969; *American Fiction, 1851-1875* (1965); *American Fiction, 1876-1900* (1966). San Marino, Calif.: Huntington Library.

"This bibliography lists American editions of prose fiction written by Americans and published between 1774 and [1900]." It includes novels, romances, tales, short stories, fictitious biographies, travels, sketches, allegories, "tract-like tales, and other writings of similar nature." The entries are arranged alphabetically under author's name when known, otherwise by title. "The first or earliest listed edition of each title entered in the bibliography is noted in the Chronological Index. The Title Index lists the titles of all entries in the main body of the work."

NOTE: Other bibliographies—of authors, periods, and topics—may be found in Section IV (Editions and Series) and Section VI (American Literature Journals).

II Literary History and Criticism

75. Aaron, Daniel. *The Unwritten War: American Writers and the Civil War.* New York: Knopf, 1973. P.

"One would expect writers, the 'antennae of the race,' to say something revealing about the meaning, if not the causes, of the War. This book argues implicitly throughout that, with a few notable exceptions, they did not. ... But whether the literary dearth is to be accounted for by the blocking out of race, the reticence of veterans, the fastidiousness of lady readers, the alleged indifference of the most gifted writers to the War itself, or simply by the general rule that national convulsions do not provide the best conditions for artistic creativeness, it can still be argued (and I shall do so) that the paucity of 'epics' and 'masterpieces' is no index of the impact of the War on American writers. As I shall seek to show, the War more than casually touched and engaged a number of writers [including Hawthorne, Whitman, Melville, Adams, James, Howells, Mark Twain, De Forest, Bierce, Tourgée, Crane, Frederic, Lanier, Cable, Faulkner], and its literary reverberations are felt to this day."

Professor Aaron's focus on the impact of the Civil War on writers thus complements Edmund Wilson's somewhat greater emphasis on the literature of the war itself in *Patriotic Gore* (**213**).

76. Ahlstrom, Sidney E. *A Religious History of the American People.* New Haven: Yale University Press, 1972.

Ahlstrom's eleven-hundred-page study attempts to discuss American religion "within the larger frame of world history," and with attention to " 'secular' movements and convictions," "the radical diversity of American religious movements," and "the social context—including its demographic, economic, political, and psychological dimensions."

77.   Aldridge, John W. *After the Lost Generation: A Critical Study of the Writers of Two Wars.* New York: McGraw-Hill, 1951. P (Noonday).

"I have been interested in tracing down such [literary] changes as have become evident since the time of Fitzgerald and Hemingway, particularly in the work of their newest successors, the younger novelists of the 1940's. In doing so, I have also inevitably written another book, a book about the two wars and their contrasting effects on the writing which the two American war generations have produced. In the main, however, the book about the disappearance of a stable society and a common set of values and the book about the two generations form a single unit and, I hope, one commentary on the same dilemma."

Aldridge discusses Hemingway, Fitzgerald, and Dos Passos as the "true literary forebears" of the "younger writers who have appeared since the end of the second war and who form, because of the war and the interval of more than twenty years, the first completely new literary generation since the generation of the 1920's: Norman Mailer, Robert Lowry, Vance Bourjaily, Merle Miller, Truman Capote, Gore Vidal, and Frederick Buechner . . . Paul Bowles, Irwin Shaw, John Horne Burns, and Alfred Hayes."

78.   Arms, George. *The Fields Were Green: A New View of Bryant, Whittier, Holmes, Lowell, and Longfellow, with a Selection of Their Poems.* Stanford, Calif.: Stanford University Press, 1953.

"American poets of the last century occupy a paradoxical place. They have unequaled currency in the national mind and their poems have constituted a large part of the formal study of American literature. Yet critical response to them is generally nonexistent, or if expressed, anti-pathetic. My belief is that there has been a failure to do justice to these poets and that in dealing with them as it does criticism is either inadequate or wrongheaded. . . . Not even a partisan could at the moment contend that Bryant, Whittier, Holmes, Lowell, and Longfellow occupy a place of any significance in the literary tradition of Western civilization. It is not my argument that they should be awarded a place at the summit. I do not claim their absolute greatness, but feel that a just consideration will cause us to appreciate these schoolroom poets as of a real literary worth.

"As a preliminary step in such appreciation we must recognize that certain differences exist between their work and that of the moderns or of many other poets of the past. Most of these differences place them at some disadvantage in my own critical view and in that of modern readers. But within these limits we can enjoy and praise much of their poetry, for the differences belong more to the realm of fashion than of principle. For example, a literary rather than a colloquial diction, the use of poetical-picturesque subject matter, and an effect of relaxation are three differences which are major drawbacks to most of us. But none of these can be regarded as elemental in literary art, and as we shall see throughout this book they need some qualification as judgments of all the work of the poets."

79.   Baker, Houston A., Jr. *Long Black Song: Essays in Black American Literature and Culture.* Charlottesville: University Press of Virginia, 1972.

These eight essays "are attempts to show the distinctiveness of black American culture and to bring into focus evidence that is essential for the critic of black American literature. Rather than paying dutiful homage to Phillis Wheatley, Jupiter Hammon, Frances Harper and a number of other less skillful early black writers, the essays examine the folklore that Frederick Douglass, David Walker, and their accomplished successors built upon. Rather than attempting to force Richard Wright into the naturalistic and proletarian traditions of white American literature, an attempt is made to discover the prime motivating forces of Wright's life and work. Rather than continuing the argument over the black man's humanity the essays acknowledge at the outset the existence of a separate and distinct culture. Such endeavors are more profitable than attempts to ignore black American culture or efforts to define its literature as the spontaneous overflow of primitive black emotions. Moreover, they are more rewarding than a struggle to force both the literature and the culture into preexistent molds that were not designed to contain them."

The book includes a selected bibliography of criticism of black American literature.

80.   Berthoff, Warner. *The Ferment of Realism: American Literature, 1884-1919.* New York: Free Press, 1965.

Quentin Anderson, in a foreword, states that a proper "history of American literature is inseparable from its culture and historical occasion." Berthoff puts it more complexly: "Literary history is coextensive with social history, cultural history, intellectual history but is not identical with any of them. . . .

Literary history ... is determined finally by the distinctive nature of the forms it examines, and these forms are unique in
being at the same time, in varying proportion: (1) works of art,
seeking self-completion; (2) documents in testimony, relating
to common consciousness of truths and probabilities; (3) acts of
expression, more or less sustained and pitched at different
intensities, in which we may see, among other things, how
language, the genetic code-matrix of historical culture, is being
'kept up.' "

81.   Bewley, Marius. *The Complex Fate: Hawthorne, Henry James, and
      Some Other American Writers.* Introd. and interpolations by F. R.
      Leavis. London: Chatto and Windus, 1952.

      Nine of the thirteen essays collected in this volume (all origi-
      nally published between 1949 and 1952 and, with one excep-
      tion, in *Scrutiny*) are devoted to Hawthorne and James, focus-
      ing on their "Americanness" and their "critical consciousness
      of the national society [in] dealing with American attitudes and
      material." The title is from Henry James: "It's a complex fate,
      being an American, and one of the responsibilities it entails is
      fighting against a superstitious valuation of Europe." See next
      entry.

82.   Bewley, Marius. *The Eccentric Design: Form in the Classic American
      Novel.* New York: Columbia University Press, 1959. P.

      This work is "an attempt to enlarge upon, to corroborate
      with additional evidence, and define more rigorously, certain
      general statements made in the opening chapter of *The Com-
      plex Fate* [e.g., 'the largest problem that confronted the artist in
      nineteenth-century America, and which still occupies him,
      might be defined as the nature of his separateness, and the
      nature of his connection with European, and particularly with
      English, culture']. [It] deals with literature in which the Ameri-
      can artist [particularly Cooper, Hawthorne, Melville, James,
      and Fitzgerald] has endeavored to confront and understand
      his own emotional and spiritual needs as an American. He
      cannot, after all, confront them as an Englishman or a Welsh-
      man. But the focus is on his achievement as an artist, not on any
      patriotic or expatriate commitments he may make."

83.   Bone, Robert. *The Negro Novel in America.* 1958. Rev. ed., New
      Haven: Yale University Press, 1965. P.

"Assimilationism and Negro nationalism, concepts indispensable to understanding the cultural history of the American Negro, are employed throughout the present work not only in interpreting the consciousness of individual authors, but in gauging the temper of whole periods. They help, for example, to unravel the conflicting impulses within the early Negro novel (1890-1920), and to illuminate the nationalist character of the Negro Renaissance (1920-30). They help to account for the success of the 'Party line' among Negro intellectuals of the 1930s, and to explain the recent trend toward 'raceless' novels in postwar Negro fiction. They provide, in short, a fixed point of reference from which to view the changing racial attitudes of the Negro novelist—attitudes which are often fundamental to the content of his art.

"It is art, in the long run, that matters.... While I have my social biases and have not hesitated to express them, I have tried to avoid the Parrington fallacy [of confusing social theory with aesthetic judgment; see **167**] by placing strong emphasis upon form—attempting to establish the work of art in its own right before viewing it as part of the cultural process."

Bone's work needs to be supplemented with more recent studies (see **62**), but it remains a useful place to begin.

84. Boorstin, Daniel J. *The Americans*. 3 vols: *The Colonial Experience* (1958), *The National Experience* (1965), and *The Democratic Experience* (1973). New York: Random House. P (Vintage).

"America began as a sobering experience. The colonies were a disproving ground for utopias. In the following chapters we will illustrate how dreams made in Europe—the dreams of the zionist, the perfectionist, the philanthropist, and the transplanter—were dissipated or transformed by the American reality. A new civilization was being born less out of plans and purposes than out of the unsettlement which the New World brought to the ways of the Old."

"A great resource of America was vagueness. American uncertainties, products of ignorance and progress, were producers of optimism and energy. Although few acknowledged it, in the era between the Revolution and the Civil War this vagueness was a source of American strength. Americans were already distinguished less by what they clearly knew or definitely believed than by their grand and fluid hopes. If other nations had been held together by common certainties, Americans were being united by a common vagueness and a common effervescence. Their first enterprise was to discover who they were, where they were, when they were, what they were capable of, and how they could expand and organize. Their America was still little more than a point of departure. The nation would long profit from having been born without ever having been conceived."

"The century after the Civil War was to be an Age of Revolution—of countless, little-noticed revolutions, which occurred not in the halls of legislatures or on battlefields or on the barricades but in homes and farms and factories and schools and stores, across the landscape and in the air—so little noticed because they came so swiftly, because they touched Americans everywhere and every day."

A social and intellectual history probably best read after Morison and Commager (**158**).

85. Booth, Wayne C. *The Rhetoric of Fiction.* Chicago: University of Chicago Press, 1961. P (Phoenix Book).

Discusses "the technique of non-didactic fiction [in American, British, and Continental works] viewed as the art of communicating with readers—the rhetorical resources available to the writer of epic, novel, or short story as he tries, consciously or unconsciously, to impose his fictional world upon the reader."

The discussion is extended and sharpened in Professor Booth's latest book, *A Rhetoric of Irony* (1974).

86. Bradbury, John M. *Renaissance in the South: A Critical History of the Literature, 1920-1960.* Chapel Hill: University of North Carolina Press, 1963.

"The Southern Literary Renaissance, some forty years old but still maturely vigorous in 1963, is a phenomenon unparalleled in American history. The country has experienced significant creative revivals in the past, principally in New England and the Midwest, but never before has a region so suddenly, so widely, and so effectively burst into literary activity as has the South since 1920."

87. Bridgman, Richard. *The Colloquial Style in America.* New York: Oxford University Press, 1966.

With emphasis on the works of Henry James, Mark Twain, Hemingway, and Gertrude Stein, Bridgman traces "a movement in colloquial prose that progressively simplifies and concentrates verbal expression" to meet the unique needs of an American audience. The sources which "supplied the motor force for a native style in the United States [were] romantic individualism, nationalistic pride, and practical necessity." The resulting colloquial style is characterized by "stress on the individual verbal unit, a resulting fragmentation of syntax, and the use of repetition to bind and unify."

88. Brooks, Van Wyck. *Makers and Finders: A History of the Writer in America, 1800-1915.* 5 vols.: *The World of Washington Irving* (1944); *The Flowering of New England, 1815-1865* (1936; P); *The Times of Melville and Whitman (1947); New England: Indian Summer, 1865-1915* (1940; P); *The Confident Years: 1885-1915* (1952). New York: Dutton.

"It was to make this [tradition] clear that I wrote *Makers and Finders*, hoping to connect the literary present with the past, reviving the special kind of memory that fertilizes the living mind and gives it the sense of a base on which to build. I had in my reading discovered traits that many of our writers possessed in common, which gave them a general character that was properly their own, and it struck me that they had contributed to a sort of common fund, a fund of similar experiences, desires, and hopes. It seemed to me that, collectively speaking, our writers formed a guild, that they had even worked for a common end,—an elevating end and deeply human—and that living writers, aware of this, could never quite feel as they had felt before, that they were working alone and working in the dark. It was never my intention to attempt to present the 'American mind,' or to write a literary history in the usual sense.... My sole criterion was style, which writers must have to rank as writers,—whether they possess 'form' or not ... and I included philosophers, economists and other expository writers along with the poets, historians, novelists and critics when, and only when, they possessed this mark."

Brooks's other works include *The Wine of the Puritans* (1908), *America's Coming-of-Age* (1915), *The Ordeal of Mark Twain* (1920), and *The Pilgrimage of Henry James* (1925).

89. Brown, Herbert Ross. *The Sentimental Novel in America, 1789-1860.* Durham, N.C.: Duke University Press, 1940.

"As a means of presenting a cross-section of the national imagination as it is revealed in the abundant outpouring of

sentimental novels, I have been primarily concerned with social trends, forces, creeds, movements, and literary fashions.
The reflection of these streams of thought is, with a few exceptions, more significant than a chronological account of authors
and novels. Many of the titles of these faded favorites, it is
charitable to remark at the threshold of this book, deserve to
appear on any list of the world's worst fiction. Collectively,
however, they represent a wide level of taste, and they have had
an enormous influence upon the lives of the American
people."

90. Cady, Edwin H. *The Light of Common Day: Realism in American
Fiction*. Bloomington: Indiana University Press, 1971.

Ten essays on realism and related topics (naturalism, romanticism, frontier humor, mock-epic) and authors (Hawthorne,
Henry James, Mark Twain, Howells, Stephen Crane, Owen
Wister), informed by the spirit of the epigraph attributed to
Michelangelo: "The best light on a statue is the light of the
common marketplace." Professor Cady concludes with a vigorous attack on Richard Chase and Leslie Fiedler, who see by
different lights. See **94** and **112**.

91. Cambon, Glauco. *The Inclusive Flame: Studies in American Poetry*.
Bloomington: Indiana University Press, 1963. P.

"Parts of this book first appeared in Italian magazines during 1955, and the book itself was published in Italy in 1956. . . .
The only addition to the work as published in 1956 is the
chapter on Robert Lowell. . . . While making no claim to completeness, my work does attempt to probe into the recurrent
American endeavor to grasp a totality of experience through
poetry—hence its present title [from Hart Crane: 'The pure
possession, the inclusive cloud whose heart is fire shall come '].
References to Italian or generally European writers will, I
hope, be taken as a tribute to the vitality of this American
endeavor. The sounding board of a culture is always larger
than the culture itself." Cambon considers especially the poetry
of Robinson, Stevens, Hart Crane, W. C. Williams, and Lowell.

92. *The Cambridge History of American Literature*. Ed. William P.
Trent et al. 4 vols. New York: Putnam's, 1917-21.

The first large-scale collaborative literary history of the
United States, the *Cambridge History* is "a survey of the life of the
American people as expressed in their writings rather than a
history of belles-lettres alone. . . .

"To write the intellectual history of America from the modern aesthetic standpoint is to miss precisely what makes it significant among modern literatures, namely, that for two centuries the main energy of Americans went into exploration, settlement, labour for subsistence, religion, and statecraft. For nearly two hundred years a people with the same traditions and with the same intellectual capacities as their contemporaries across the sea found themselves obliged to dispense for the most part with art for art. But the long inhibition and belated expansion of their purely aesthetic impulses, unfavourable as it was to the development of poetry and fiction, was no serious handicap to the production of a prose competently recording their practical activities and expressing their moral, religious, and political ideas.

"For the nineteenth century, too, without neglecting the writers of imaginative literature who have been most emphasized by our literary historians, we have attempted to do a new service by giving a place in our record to departments of literature, such as travels, oratory, memoirs, which have lain somewhat out of the main tradition of literary history but which may be, as they are in the United States, highly significant of the national temper."

A standard work in its day, the *Cambridge History* (and its accompanying bibliographies) has been largely eclipsed by the *Literary History of the United States* (**194** and **58**)—but not totally obscured, as the thirty-second printing in 1969 attests.

93. Cash, Wilbur J. *The Mind of the South*. New York: Knopf, 1941. P (Vintage).

"Proud, brave, honorable by its lights, courteous, personally generous, loyal, swift to act, often too swift, but signally effective, sometimes terrible, in its action—such was the South at its best. And such at its best it remains today, despite the great falling away in some of its virtues. Violence, intolerance, aversion and suspicion toward new ideas, an incapacity for analysis, an inclination to act from feeling rather than from thought, an exaggerated individualism and a too narrow concept of social responsibility, attachment to fictions and false values, above all too great attachment to racial values and a tendency to justify cruelty and injustice in the name of those values, sentimentality and a lack of realism—these have been its characteristic vices in the past. And, despite changes for the better, they remain its characteristic vices today."

94.   Chase, Richard. *The American Novel and Its Tradition*. Garden
City, N.Y.: Doubleday, 1957. P (Anchor Book).

"Since the earliest days the American novel, in its most original and characteristic form, has worked out its destiny and
defined itself by incorporating an element of romance....
[But] the best American novelists have found uses for romance
far beyond the escapism, fantasy, and sentimentality often
associated with it. They have found that in the very freedom of
romance from the conditions of actuality there are certain
potential virtues of the mind, which may be suggested by such
words as rapidity, irony, abstraction, profundity. These qualities have made romance a suitable, even, as it seems, an inevitable, vehicle for the moral and intellectual ideas of American
novelists." Chase's study is arranged chronologically with chapters on Charles Brockden Brown, Cooper, Hawthorne, Melville, Henry James, Mark Twain, Norris, and Faulkner. See **90**.

95.   Clark, Harry Hayden, ed. *Transitions in American Literary History*. Durham, N.C.: Duke University Press, 1954.

"In the present work we have used [the terms *neoclassicism,
romanticism,* and *realism*] not as representing anything static or
absolute but rather as representing somewhat flexible centers
of emphasis with widening circles of departure from such
centers." The main problem investigated is "how and especially
why American literature did change historically from one
[such] center of emphasis to another." Thus the main concern
is "not with the periods at the time of their most typical development but with the 'in-between' periods" which reveal the
cause and effect of change.

The volume is an outgrowth and a continuation of the critical inquiry begun in *The Reinterpretation of American Literature*
(**114**). Included are an introduction by Clark and essays by C.
H. Faust, Leon Howard, M. F. Heiser, G. H. Orians, Alexander
Kern, Floyd Stovall, and Robert Falk.

96.   Cohen, Hennig, ed. *The American Experience* and *The American
Culture*. Both subtitled *Approaches to the Study of the United States*.
Boston: Houghton Mifflin, 1968. P.

These companion volumes reprint sixty-three articles on
American studies which originally appeared in the journal
American Quarterly (**333**).

The American Experience "approaches the American experience loosely, pragmatically and from a variety of disciplines

and methodologies—alone and in combinations—starting with efforts to define the national character. Its categories include the past and its uses, the crucial encounter of innocence and experience, an example of the force and complexity of political thought, the national hero and the interplay of American culture and the cultures of other nationalities. The collection concludes with essays that focus on methods of studying the American experience." *The American Culture*, "more contemporary in its emphasis, provides a wide sampling of the methods and subject matter of American Studies scholarship. Its sub-headings are 'Images and Myths,' 'Ideas,' 'Machines,' 'Mass Society' and 'Varieties of Cultural Experience.' " Cf. **113, 116, 139, 152.**

97. Cohen, Hennig, ed. *Landmarks of American Writing*. New York: Basic Books, 1969.

Thirty-two essays by different scholars on significant American works originally prepared for the Voice of America "Forum" Series.

98. Commager, Henry Steele. *The American Mind: An Interpretation of American Thought and Character since the 1880's*. New Haven: Yale University Press, 1950. P (Yale; Bantam).

"If the eighteenth-century titles were still fashionable, I would call this book Prolegomenon to an Interpretation of Some Aspects of American Thought and Character from the 1880's to the 1940's. . . . I am not concerned here with abbreviated histories of American philosophy or religion, sociology or economics, politics or law, but with ideas that illuminate the American mind and ways of using ideas that illustrate the American character. . . . The far from inarticulate major premise of my investigation is that there is a distinctively American way of thought, character, and conduct." Contains extensive bibliographies.

99. Cowie, Alexander. *The Rise of the American Novel*. New York: American Book Co., 1948.

"This volume presents materials for a critical history of the American novel from the beginning to the latter part of the nineteenth century, together with a concluding chapter intended as a rough indication of developments to [1940]. . . . [It] attempts to indicate the evolution of the American novel by means of comparatively full treatments of representative writers: all the major novelists, most of the secondary figures, and a considerable sprinkling of writers whose absolute value is very slight."

100. Cowley, Malcolm, ed. *After the Genteel Tradition: American Writers, 1910-1930.* Carbondale: Southern Illinois University Press, 1964.

A revised and expanded version of the collection originally published in 1937 (subtitled *American Writers since 1910*). Sixteen essays on individual writers by various hands in the spirit of Sinclair Lewis' 1930 Nobel Prize address: "clear[ing] the trail from Victorian and Howellsian timidity and gentility in American fiction to honesty and boldness and passion of life." Includes "A Literary Calendar: 1911-1930."

101. Cowley, Malcolm. *Exile's Return: A Literary Odyssey of the 1920's.* 1934. Rev. ed., New York: Viking, 1951. P (Compass Book).

"This book is the story to 1930 of what used to be called the lost generation of American writers. It was Gertrude Stein who first applied the phrase to them. 'You are all a lost generation,' she said to Ernest Hemingway, and Hemingway used the remark as an inscription for his first novel. It was a good novel and became a craze—young men tried to get as imperturbably drunk as the hero, young women of good families took a succession of lovers in the same heartbroken fashion as the heroine, they all talked like Hemingway characters and the name was fixed. . . .

"I am speaking of the young men and women [Hemingway, Fitzgerald, Pound, Eliot, Cummings, Hart Crane, and others] who graduated from college, or might have graduated, between 1915, say, and 1922. They were never united into a single group or school. Instead they included several loosely defined and vaguely hostile groups, in addition to many individuals who differed with every group among their contemporaries; the fact is that all of them differed constantly with all the others. They all felt, however, a sharper sense of difference in regard to writers older than themselves who hadn't shared their adventures. It was as if the others had never undergone the same initiatory rites and had never been admitted to the same broad confraternity. In a strict sense the new writers formed what is known as a literary generation." See next entry.

102. Cowley, Malcolm. *A Second Flowering: Works and Days of the Lost Generation*. New York: Viking, 1973. P (Compass Book).

Cowley's further discovery of the lost generation, told in terms of eight representative figures—Fitzgerald, Hemingway, Dos Passos, Cummings, Wilder, Faulkner, Wolfe, and Hart Crane. "That particular age group [i.e., born between 1894 and 1900] had more in common and was more conscious of possessing shared purposes than the group that preceded or followed it. . . . They were all extraordinary persons. I have dealt with their early dreams of the literary life, their subsequent careers at home and abroad, and the works they produced during a period that now seems to have been a second flowering of American literature.

103. Cowley, Malcolm. *Think Back on Us . . .: A Contemporary Chronicle of the 1930's*. Ed. Henry Dan Piper. 2 vols.: *The Social Record* and *The Literary Record*. Carbondale: Southern Illinois University Press, 1972. P.

Two volumes which collect essays, reviews, and editorials written by Cowley when he was literary editor of the *New Republic* in the 1930s.

104. Crèvecoeur, J. Hector St. John de. *Letters from an American Farmer: Describing Certain Provincial Situations, Manners, and Customs, Not Generally Known; and Conveying Some Idea of the Late and Present Interior Circumstances of the British Colonies in North America. Written for the Information of a Friend in England, by J. Hector St. John, A Farmer in Pennsylvania*. London, 1782. Rpt. New York: Dutton, 1957. P.

Actually written by a French émigré named Michel-Guillaume Jean de Crèvecoeur at his New York farm, the twelve essays provide sketches of prerevolutionary life in rural America.

"What is an American?" Crèvecoeur asks, in a rhapsodic passage, that, while characteristic, perhaps does not do full justice to the variety and complexity of his ideas: "Here are no aristocratical families, no courts, no kings, no bishops, no ecclesiastical dominion, no invisible power giving to a few a very visible one; no great manufacturers employing thousands, no great refinements of luxury. The rich and the poor are not so far removed from each other as they are in Europe. Some few towns excepted, we are all tillers of the

earth, from Nova Scotia to West Florida. We are a people of
cultivators, scattered over an immense territory, communicating with each other by means of good roads and navigable
rivers, united by the silken bands of mild government, all
respecting the laws, without dreading their power, because
they are equitable. We are all animated with the spirit of an
industry which is unfettered and unrestrained, because each
person works for himself. If [an Englishman] travels through
our rural districts he views not the hostile castle, and the
haughty mansion, contrasted with the clay-built hut and mis-
erable cabin, where cattle and men help to keep each other
warm, and dwell in meanness, smoke, and indigence. A pleas-
ing uniformity of decent competence appears throughout
our habitations. The meanest of our log-houses is a dry and
comfortable habitation. Lawyer or merchant are the fairest
titles our towns afford; that of a farmer is the only appella-
tion of the rural inhabitants of our country. . . . We have no
princes, for whom we toil, starve, and bleed: we are the most
perfect society now existing in the world."

Crèvecoeur was also the author of *Voyage dans la Haute
Pensylvanie et dans l'Etat de New-York* (1801) and *Sketches of
Eighteenth-Century America* (first published in 1925).

105. Cunliffe, Marcus. *The Literature of the United States.* 1954. 3rd.
ed., rev., Baltimore: Penguin, 1970. P.

"A small book on a large topic," as Cunliffe readily admits,
but one which surveys perceptively the major American authors "while uneasily aware that they are not the only pebbles
on the beach."

106. Curti, Merle. *The Growth of American Thought.* 1943. 3rd ed.,
New York: Harper, 1964.

"In [the colonial] period Europeans adapted their heritage
of thought and knowledge to the conditions of colonization
and to a new physical and social environment." This was
followed in the eighteenth century by "cultural nationalism,
the expanding Enlightenment, and the conservative reac-
tion. . . . The first third of the nineteenth century, roughly,
was marked by patrician leadership in thought. This, however, was challenged by the frontier in those decades. . . . The
period extending approximately from 1830 to 1850 was
dominated by the democratic upheaval that profoundly affected intellectual life. . . . This was also the golden day of

progress and optimism, in which science and technology made great advances, in which knowledge was popularized. . . .

"The period extending roughly from 1850 to 1870 was marked by the triumph of nationalism and business ideology in social and political thought. . . . From 1870 or thereabouts to the end of the century the dominant idea was the assertion of individualism in a corporate age of applied science. Science advanced on supernaturalism, and evolutionary thought affected and was affected by the utilitarian ideas and interests that prevailed. . . . The imperialistic adventure of 1898 and subsequent years and the crusade of 1917 to make the world safe for democracy were followed by disillusionment, criticism, and complacency, and then by renewed optimism in the decade of the 'twenties. But the breakdown in economy during the 'thirties eventuated in new intellectual searches, and the world crisis intensified the widespread pessimism and uncertainty."

107. Dorson, Richard M. *American Folklore*. Chicago: University of Chicago Press, 1959. P.

"The scientific folklorist seeks out, observes, collects, and describes the inherited traditions of the community, whatsoever forms they take. . . . The current approaches are those of the comparative folklorists, who are primarily Europe-centered; cultural anthropologists, who are chiefly concerned with non-literate peoples; special pleaders, following in the steps of Sir James Frazer and his *Golden Bough*, and now Freud and Jung, who would interpret all folklore in the light of one universal theme; regional collectors, who drift into parochialism; literary scholars untrained in folklore; folksong and folk music specialists; and popularizers and entertainers. No overarching synthesis has integrated the study of folklore with the history of American civilization. It is my conviction that the only meaningful approach to the folk traditions of the United States must be made against the background of American history, with its unique circumstances and environment. What other history—or folklore—grapples in the same measure with the factors of colonization, immigration, Negro slavery, the westward movement, or mass culture?

"If folklore scholars are not yet united by a general theory for American folklore, they fully agree on the methods necessary for accurate collecting and documenting of folk materials. Texts must be secured literally from informants; full background information should be provided on these human sources of folklore; all traditions, whether collected currently in the field, or excavated from the printed sources of an earlier day, need to be verified through the great indexes and reference works which form the scientific tools of the folklorist. Only with these proofs can we be reasonably sure of the oral, traditional character of our assumed folklore.

"The present book thus rests on a special theory for American folklore and a general method for all folklore. Its outline follows the broad sweep of American history, and its materials come from authentic collections and studies."

Professor Dorson's other works include *Jonathan Draws the Long Bow* (New England folklore; 1946); *America Begins: Early American Writing* (1950); *Buying the Wind: Regional Folklore in the United States* (1964); *American Negro Folktales* (1967); *American Folklore and the Historian* (1971); *Folklore: Selected Essays* (1972); and *America in Legend: Folklore from the Colonial Period to the Present* (1973).

108. Downer, Alan S. *Fifty Years of American Drama, 1900-1950.* Chicago: Henry Regnery Co., 1951. P.

"The following essay is not intended as a history of the American Drama in its most productive years. Rather it is an attempt to analyze the product: where it came from, how it developed, and where it arrived. It involves, therefore, the inclusion of plays of varying worth, and the omission of many of both historical interest and aesthetic value.

"I have written in terms of plays rather than playwrights, since my interest is in dramatic art rather than individual achievement. . . . The chapter divisions may seem arbitrary; they are intended to organize the material in terms of dramatic form (representational and presentational) and of subject matter (folk drama and comedy) most typical of America."

See also Professor Downer's edition of essays on the development of modern American drama entitled *American Drama and Its Critics* (1965).

109. Emerson, Everett, ed. *Major Writers of Early American Literature.* Madison: University of Wisconsin Press, 1972.

"The transplantation of Western culture to a new land

opened up exciting possibilities. What kinds of creations was the new country to produce? What were the distinctive qualities of the American experience? The essays that follow [on Bradford, Bradstreet, Edward Taylor, Cotton Mather, William Byrd, Edwards, Franklin, Freneau, and Charles Brockden Brown; by different scholars] supply answers to these questions. Knowledge of early American literature has often been limited to a few generalizations about the Puritan Mind, the American Enlightenment, and the development of literary nationalism. This volume provides a solid foundation for an intelligent appreciation of the beginnings of American literature."

110. Feidelson, Charles, Jr. *Symbolism and American Literature.* Chicago: University of Chicago Press, 1953. P (Phoenix Book).

A study of Hawthorne, Whitman, Melville, and Poe (as descended from Emerson): "It is likely that the really vital common denominator is precisely their attitude toward their medium—that their distinctive quality is a devotion to the possibilities of symbolism. . . . [They] inherited the basic problem of romanticism: the vindication of imaginative thought in a world grown abstract and material; and their solution . . . is closer to modern notions of symbolic reality than to romantic egoism. Considered as pure romantics they are minor disciples of European masters. Their symbolistic method is their title to literary independence."

111. Feidelson, Charles, Jr., and Paul Brodtkorb, Jr., eds. *Interpretations of American Literature.* New York: Oxford University Press, 1959. P.

"This is a collection of [twenty-three] interpretive essays on major works, major writers, and a few major strains of American literature" by well-known critics, concentrating on Hawthorne, Melville, Emerson, Whitman, Mark Twain, James, Hemingway, and Faulkner.

112. Fiedler, Leslie A. *Love and Death in the American Novel.* 1960. Rev. ed., New York: Stein and Day, 1966. P (Dell).

"American literature is distinguished by the number of dangerous and disturbing books in its canon—and American scholarship by its ability to conceal this fact. To redeem our great books from the commentaries on them is one of the

chief functions of this study.... I have attempted in the
present study to emphasize the neglected contexts of American fiction, largely depth-psychological and anthropological,
but sociological and formal as well.... The failure of the
American fictionist to deal with adult heterosexual love and
his consequent obsession with death, incest and innocent
homosexuality are not merely matters of historical interest or
literary relevance. They affect the lives we lead from day to
day and influence the writers in whom the consciousness of
our plight is given clarity and form." This is a book which
tamer critics call "provocative," by which they mean Fiedler is
wrongheaded but still formidable or that he is alternately
perceptive and outrageous. Part of the provocation is "the
lack of footnotes and formal bibliography [which] will advise
the wary that I have sought everywhere the kind of validity
which depends not on faithfulness to 'fact' but on insight and
sensitivity to nuance." See **90**.

Professor Fiedler sees *Love and Death in the American Novel* as
one section of a trilogy—along with *Waiting for the End* (1964)
and *The Return of the Vanishing American* (1968)—"the first of
whose parts concerns itself with *eros* and *thanatos*; the second,
with the hope of apocalypse and its failure; the third, with the
Indian—all three, as I hope becomes clear in this volume, with
that peculiar form of madness which dreams, and achieves,
and *is* the true West." Fiedler has also written *An End to
Innocence: Essays on Culture and Politics* (1955), *No! In Thunder*
(1960), and *Collected Essays* (2 vols., 1971).

113. Fishwick, Marshall W., ed. *American Studies in Transition*. Boston: Houghton Mifflin, 1964. P.

Contains eighteen essays which "fall into three main
categories. The first group centers on ways of understanding
America; the second on ways of teaching whatever clues and
conclusions our scholarship uncovers; and the third on the
impact of American Studies and policies abroad." Cf. **96, 116,
139, 152**.

114. Foerster, Norman, ed. *The Reinterpretation of American Literature: Some Contributions toward the Understanding of Its Historical
Development*. New York: Harcourt, Brace, 1928. Reissued,
with a new preface by Robert P. Falk, New York: Russell &
Russell, 1959.

Nine essays by various scholars written in the dark days

when American literature was merely "a hobby that may be tolerated" in departments of English. Nevertheless, Professors Pattee, Foerster, Hubbell, H. M. Jones, Murdock, Parrington, and H. H. Clark had their eyes on the dawn. "The time is not distant, however, when this study [of American literature] will be pursued in the same spirit and with the same methods employed in the study of other modern literatures. That such a change in spirit and method will involve a reinterpretation of our literary history is, I think, demonstrated by this book. Its object is not to present striking discoveries and novel conclusions, but to suggest the spirit and manner in which a fresh interpretation should be undertaken."

115. Fussell, Edwin. *Frontier: American Literature and the American West*. Princeton, N.J.: Princeton University Press, 1965. P.

"The simple truth is that the American West was neither more nor less interesting than any other place, except in mythology or in the swollen egos of Westerners, until by interpretation the great American writers—all of whom happened to be Eastern—made it seem so. This they did by conceiving its physical aspects (forests, rivers, lakes, clearings, settlements, prairies, plains, deserts) and its social aspects (isolation, simplicity, improvisation, criticism, chaos, restlessness, paradox, irony) as expressive emblems for the invention and development of a new national civilization, and not as things in themselves." Fussell traces the development and decline of this "frontier metaphor" in the works of Cooper, Hawthorne, Poe, Thoreau, Melville, and Whitman.

116. Hague, John A., ed. *American Character and Culture: Some Twentieth Century Perspectives*. DeLand, Fla.: Everett Edwards Press, 1964.

Ten essays which attempt to furnish an "overview of some of the striking new developments which have resulted from interdisciplinary studies in the past fifteen years." Cf. **96, 113, 139, 152**.

117. Hart, James D. *The Popular Book: A History of America's Literary Taste*. New York: Oxford University Press, 1950. P (University of California Press).

A survey, from colonial times to 1949, of "the books most widely read in America in the years immediately following their publication." Hart attempts to trace the relationship between the books the nation preferred and social and historical factors which may have influenced the preferences. Includes a bibliographical checklist and a chronological index of books discussed in the text. Cf. **160** and **165**.

118.   Hassan, Ihab. *Contemporary American Literature, 1945-1972: An Introduction*. New York: Ungar, 1973. P.

"I intend this book, modestly and briefly, as an introduction to contemporary American [fiction, poetry, and drama] though it makes no claim of completeness. It may also provide a critical sense of the literature in question. . . . The writers [discussed] here all began to publish during or after World War II. Almost all of them are born after the year 1910, which I have taken as a plausible cut-off point. . . .

"A general introduction limns the character of the period, which is also reflected in its non-fiction and criticism. Chapters on fiction, poetry, and drama then follow. Each chapter begins with a short introduction, moving from portraits of major and prominent authors, in chronological sequence, to glimpses of significant types and trends." Includes a bibliography.

119.   Hassan, Ihab. *Radical Innocence: Studies in the Contemporary American Novel*. Princeton, N.J.: Princeton University Press, 1961.

"The contemporary self recoils, *from* the world, *against* itself. It has discovered absurdity. . . . Yet if the contemporary self is in recoil, it is not, we hope and believe, cravenly on the run. Its *recoil* is one of the resources of its awareness, a strategy of its *will*." Primarily concerned with American novelists "whose achievement came to public attention after World War II."

120.   Hicks, Granville. *The Great Tradition: An Interpretation of American Literature since the Civil War*. 1933. Rev. ed., New York: Macmillan, 1935. P (Quadrangle).

"What stirs us in Emerson is his confidence in the common man, his courageous appeal for action, his faith in the future. He and Thoreau were rebels against the shams and oppressions of their day. They used the language of their times, the language of individualism, but they spoke for all the oppressed, and some of their words remain a call to arms. Whitman felt deeply his kinship with the workers and farmers and caught a glimpse of the collective society. Howells, James, and Mark Twain shrank in their various ways from the cupidity of the gilded age, and Howells, teaching himself to think in terms of a new social order, tried, however feebly, to create, in imagination and fact, a better world. Garland and Norris denounced oppression; Herrick and Phillips worked for reform; Sinclair and London called themselves socialists.

"This is the great tradition of American literature. Ours has been a critical literature, critical of greed, cowardice, and meanness. It has been a hopeful literature, touched again and again with a passion for brotherhood, justice, and intellectual honesty. That the writers of the past could not have conceived of the revolutionary literature of today and would, perhaps, repudiate it if they were alive, makes no difference. We see that the fulfillment of their ideals involves far more than they realized. It involves not merely fulfilling but also transcending their vision. It involves not merely criticism but destruction of capitalism and its whole way of life."

Hicks resigned from the Communist party in 1939, as a result of the disillusionment he discussed in *Where We Came Out* (1954). See Daniel Aaron's *Writers on the Left: Episodes in American Literary Communism* (1961). Cf. **180**.

121. Hoffman, Daniel G. *Form and Fable in American Fiction*. New York: Oxford University Press, 1961. P (Norton).

A study of Irving, Hawthorne, Melville, Mark Twain, and their use of the romance. "In defining the empirical, improvised, and individual characteristics of their unique fictional forms I explore the reliance of these authors upon allegory, Gothicism, didactic, religious and travel writings, and traditions of folklore, popular culture, and mythology. . . . [These] contribute not only to the materials of the romance but also to its methods and form."

122. Hoffman, Frederick J. *The Modern Novel in America*. 1951. Rev. ed., Chicago: Henry Regnery Co., 1963. P.

Hoffman "examines the history of the twentieth-century American novel in terms of the two primary issues involved in its progress"—a Jamesian concern for "technique and method together with their implications for the development of a critical aesthetic of the novel" and a naturalistic emphasis on "the social relevance of a novel's materials, its philosophical grounding in a view of man and society, and the consequent discussion of a novelist's social responsibilities."

Coverage is of major figures from James and Howells to Hemingway and Faulkner.

123. Hoffman, Frederick J. *The Twenties: American Writing in the Postwar Decade*. 1955. Rev. ed., New York: Macmillan, 1962. P (Free Press).

"If literature is important to history, it is not because it serves as a social document or as a footnote to political or intellectual history, but primarily because it is a culmination, a genuine means of realizing the major issues of its time. With this truth in mind, I tried to see the 1920s from the perspective of its literature; and I selected for each of the book's eight chapters a literary text which I felt would serve best to present in a sharp and meaningful way the issues, concerns, and points of view discussed in it."

124. Hofstadter, Richard. *Anti-Intellectualism in American Life*. 1963. Rpt. New York: Knopf, 1966. P (Vintage Book).

"Although this book deals mainly with certain aspects of the remoter American past, it was conceived in response to the political and intellectual conditions of the 1950's. During that decade the term *anti-intellectualism*, only rarely heard before, became a familiar part of our national vocabulary of self-recrimination and intramural abuse. . . . What I have done is merely to use the idea of anti-intellectualism as a device for looking at various aspects, hardly the most appealing, of American society and culture."

125. Hofstadter, Richard. *Social Darwinism in American Thought*. 1944. Rev. ed., Boston: Beacon Press, 1955. P.

"Darwinism was seized upon as a welcome addition, perhaps the most powerful of all, to the store of ideas to which solid and conservative men appealed when they wished to reconcile their fellows to some of the hardships of life and to prevail upon them not to support hasty and ill-considered reforms. Darwinism was one of the great informing insights in this long phase in the history of the conservative mind in America. It was those who wished to defend the political status quo, above all the laissez-faire conservatives, who were first to pick up the instruments of social argument that were forged out of the Darwinian concepts. Only later, only after a style of social thought that can be called 'social Darwinism' had taken clear and recognizable form, did the dissenters from this point of view move into the arena with formidable arguments."

126. Holman, C. Hugh. *The Roots of Southern Writing: Essays on the Literature of the American South*. Athens: University of Georgia Press, 1972.

    Seventeen essays on William Gilmore Simms, Ellen Glasgow, Thomas Wolfe, Faulkner, Flannery O'Connor, and others.

127. Horton, Rod W., and Herbert W. Edwards. *Backgrounds of American Literary Thought*. 1952. 2nd ed., New York: Appleton-Century-Crofts, 1967. P.

    "The purpose of this book is to provide in compact and relatively simplified form ... the intellectual, social, political, and economic currents underlying our literature."

128. Howard, John Tasker. *Our American Music: A Comprehensive History from 1620 to the Present*. 1931. 4th ed., New York: Thomas Y. Crowell Co., 1965.

    "This book is an account of the music that has been written in America; not a history of musical activities, except, of course, where we must have some idea of the conditions that have produced the composers of each era. ... [For the purposes of this discussion] a composer is an American if, by birth or choice of permanent residence, he becomes identified with American life and institutions before his talents have had their greatest outlet; and through his associations and sympathies he makes a genuine contribution to our cultural development."

    This nine-hundred-page work includes an eighty-page bibliography. An abridged version, *A Short History of Music in America*, was written in collaboration with George Kent Bellows and published in 1957 (rev. ed., 1967; P [Apollo Edition]).

129. Howard, Leon. *Literature and the American Tradition*. New York: Doubleday, 1960.

    The first two centuries of America, when the national character was in the process of formation, produced little pure literature in the conventional sense of the word; whereas the canon of literature for the last half century, at least, is so unsettled that it is impossible to determine which authors reflect the values which posterity will call 'permanent.' Only in the middle period was there a solid body of writing beneath which one could perceive a dominant and reasonably consis-

tent moving impulse. Accordingly I was forced to divide my
investigation into three major sections. The first followed the
pattern of what is often called intellectual history. The second
consisted of somewhat conventional literary interpretation.
The third is an exploration of the mass of recent writing in an
effort to see whether my interpretation of the earlier period
revealed a force of sufficiently enduring character to continue into the present the recognizable power of the past."

Also of interest is Professor Howard's *The Connecticut Wits*
(1943), on John Trumbull, Timothy Dwight, David Hum-
phreys, and Joel Barlow.

130.   Howard, Richard. *Alone with America: Essays on the Art of Poetry
in the United States since 1950*. New York: Atheneum, 1969. P.

"In the forty-one studies which follow, an accounting is
made of American poets who, with the publication of at least
two volumes, have come into a characteristic and—as I see
it—consequential identity since the time, say, of the Korean
War. In the preceding period—between Pearl Harbor, say,
and Hiroshima—six poets had 'surfaced' to a critical assess-
ment which has been, often enough, a matter indeed of sur-
faces, but which has nonetheless established them at least as
types and at best as particulars in our literary landscape:
Berryman, Bishop, Jarrell, Lowell, Roethke and Wilbur. . . .
The poetry I wish to consider entertains a dialectical
relation—acknowledged, disputed, *endured*—with the typical
work of these six."

Richard Howard, himself a poet, discusses in individual
essays the work of forty-one contemporary American poets,
from Ammons, Ashbery, and Bly to Wagoner, Weiss, and
Wright. For the source of his title, see **153**.

131.   Hubbell, Jay B. *The South in American Literature, 1607-1900*.
Durham, N.C.: Duke University Press, 1954.

"The literature of the South has long occupied a somewhat
anomalous place in our literary histories. For many years
those Southerners who wrote about it were less concerned
with appraising its literary values than with using it to refute
the Abolitionist notion that the South was a semibarbarous
region with no claim to cultural importance. In books and
articles which prejudiced many scholars against any sectional
approach to the study of our literature they not only over-
rated Southern writers, but they also charged Northern critics
and literary historians with deliberately neglecting them.

Neglect there undoubtedly was forty years ago, but it was seldom intentional. The earlier Northern literary historians, it is true, were definitely influenced by the Abolitionist conception which they had unconsciously absorbed; and some of them may be said to have mistaken the literature of New England and New York for the literature of the United States."

See also Professor Hubbell's *South and Southwest: Literary Essays and Reminiscences* (1965) and *Who Are the Major American Writers? A Study of the Changing Literary Canon* (1972).

132. James, Henry. *The Art of the Novel: Critical Prefaces by Henry James*. Ed. Richard P. Blackmur. New York: Scribner's, 1934. P.

Eighteen prefaces written for the New York edition of his writings (Scribner's, 1907-9) which are, as James wrote to Howells, "in general, a sort of plea for Criticism, for Discrimination, for Appreciation on other than infantile lines—as against the so almost universal Anglo-Saxon absence of these things; which tends so, in our general trade, it seems to me, to break the heart."

133. Jones, Howard Mumford. *O Strange New World–American Culture: The Formative Years*. New York: Viking, 1964. P.

"The only claim I can make to originality is, I fear, the originality of synthesis. We have accumulated in American studies a frightening number of monographs and other special studies, but despite the activities of the American Studies Association we do not seem able to set these studies in the context of general Western culture nor to make of them an understandable whole. Some scholars have tried to solve the problem of multitudinousness by the adoption of the mythic method, if it be one, so that we have a number of books, excellent but limited, concerning the American Adam or the quest for Paradise or the loss of innocence.... I shall be content if these pages bring us back to the profound and central truth that American culture arises from the interplay of two great sets of forces—the Old World and the New. The Old World projected into the New a rich, complex, and contradictory set of habits, forces, practices, values, and presuppositions; and the New World accepted, modified, or rejected these or fused them with inventions of its own. That is why I have begun with the vague, vast image of the New World as seen through the European imagination, gradually narrowed my view to North America, and eventually confined myself to the United States [up to the 1840s]."

Professor Jones continues his cultural and intellectual history of America in *The Age of Energy: Varieties of American Experience, 1865-1915* (1970) in which, attempting to find a "leading principle that might serve to make sense out of American development as a whole from the age of Andrew Jackson to the presidency of Woodrow Wilson," he "hit upon the idea of energy as being central. . . . After Appomattox it was as if the enormous energy concentrated by the Civil War, not satisfied with killing or wounding a million men or more, could not check itself at the peace but went on to gigantic verbal clashes over reconstruction, industry, politics, and theology. Never was oratory more orotund, propaganda more reckless, denunciation more bitter, reform more strident—until now."

134.   Jones, Howard Mumford. *The Theory of American Literature.* 1948. Reissued with a new concluding chapter and revised bibliography, Ithaca, N.Y.: Cornell University Press, 1965. P.

"Since this study [of the problem of American literary history] was first published, an astonishing revolution has occurred in writings about American literature. Up to 1948 discussions of what makes literature American had evolved in a straight line. This evolution culminated in the *Literary History of the United States*[**194**], a book that tried to do in a more thorough way what literary historians had been attempting since John Neal published his essays on American writers in 1824 and 1825. For a century and a quarter literary historians had sought to fit their notions of a republican literature into their notions of the American republic. Although such efforts have not ceased entirely, they have become so minor a strain in the last two decades of literary theorizing as to be negligible.

"Questions of literary nationalism have been replaced by systems of interpretation essentially unhistorical in character that rest upon ideas borrowed from theories of non-rational psychology. Living critics and literary historians now tend to interpret American literary history in terms of these predilections—something political historians have not done, or have not done in the same degree. In addition, provincialism has vanished; that is, nationalism in American writing is either taken for granted or is set aside as a pseudo-problem. Consequently, American writing is now commonly looked upon not as the product of the unique experience of a people living in a representative republic, but mainly as a branch of Western literature or of the literature of 'modern' man. One can therefore argue either that the American dream has been universalized or that it has disappeared, and sometimes the same writer says both. In order to sketch this movement (which I find provocative but a little dismaying to someone who believes that the republic is founded on the ideas of Thomas Jefferson and not on those of Sigmund Freud and Carl Jung), and to place it in the context of an evolving theory of American literature, I have added a chapter, 'Postscript, 1965,' to the original edition."

135. Kazin, Alfred. *Bright Book of Life: American Novelists and Storytellers from Hemingway to Mailer*. Boston: Little, Brown, 1973. P (Dell).

   While parts of these nine essays were published previously, Kazin views the whole as "an integrated account of the fiction written in the United States since the outset of World War II." He discusses Hemingway, Faulkner, Walker Percy, Mailer, Vonnegut, Cozzens, Updike, Bellow, Malamud, Philip Roth, Issac Bashevis Singer, Katherine Anne Porter, Joyce Carol Oates, Capote, Baldwin, Ellison, Pynchon, Nabokov, William Burroughs, Cheever, McCullers, Flannery O'Connor, Salinger, Sontag, Robert Penn Warren, and others.

   In addition to *On Native Grounds* (see next entry), other works by Kazin include two collections of critical essays: *The Inmost Leaf* (1955) and *Contemporaries* (1962).

136. Kazin, Alfred. *On Native Grounds: An Interpretation of Modern American Prose Literature*. New York: Harcourt, Brace, 1942. P (Doubleday Anchor Book, abridged with a new postscript, 1956).

   "Our modern literature was rooted in those dark years of the 1880's and 1890's when all America stood suddenly between one moral order and another, and the sense of impending change became oppressive in its vividness. . . . Above all it was rooted in the need to learn what the reality of life was in the modern era." The volume is divided into three sections: "The Search for Reality (1890-1917)," "The Great Liberation (1918-1929)," and "The Literature of Crisis (1930-1940)."

137. Kouwenhoven, John A. *The Arts in Modern American Civiliza-tion.* New York: Norton, 1967. P. Originally published in 1948 as *Made in America: The Arts in Modern Civilization.*

"Though art in America is American it is singularly less so than acts and institutions which embody our history. Fruitful as the study of the interrelationship between American and European art can be, therefore, it clearly must abandon the theory that one is merely a maimed offshoot of the other. . . . As a nation we have often been hesitant and apologetic about whatever has been made in America in the vernacular tradi-tion. Perhaps the time has come when more of us are ready to accept the challenge offered to the creative imagination by the techniques and forms which first arose among our own people in our own land."

138. Krutch, Joseph Wood. *The American Drama since 1918: An Informal History.* 1939. Rev. ed., New York: Brazillier, 1957.

"Just before the First World War the American drama came suddenly to life. During the immediate postwar years our new plays began for the first time to be widely and successfully produced in the major European countries and for a time, indeed, they all but dominated the European stage. Since 1918 we have had a succession of playwrights who deserve to be called 'serious' in a sense that few of their predecessors do, and we are still part of the tradition which was established then.

"This book is an attempt to describe them as a group, to define differences and to trace trends. Its method is selective rather than inclusive but it aims to omit no playwrights who seem to the author of more than very temporary significance. The major part of it was written and published just before the outbreak of the Second World War, but a section has been added to continue the story up to the end of 1956."

Among Professor Krutch's many books are *Modernism in Modern Drama* (1954) and *The Modern Temper* (1929), which was retempered in *The Measure of Man* (1954) and *Human Nature and the Human Condition* (1959).

139. Kwiat, Joseph J., and Mary C. Turpie, eds. *Studies in American Culture: Dominant Ideas and Images.* Minneapolis: University of Minnesota Press, 1960.

Fifteen essays which attempt to give a "sense of the direc-tions that work in the general field of American culture has been taking within the past decade or so"; collected as a tribute to Professor Tremaine McDowell upon his retirement as chairman (1945-58) of the pioneering Program in American Studies at the University of Minnesota. Cf. **96, 113, 116, 152**.

140.   Larkin, Oliver W. *Art and Life in America*. 1949. Rev. and enl. ed., New York: Holt, Rinehart and Winston, 1960.

"An introductory survey of the history of architecture, sculpture, painting, and to some degree of the so-called 'minor arts' in the United States."

141.   Lawrence, D. H. *Studies in Classic American Literature*. New York: Thomas Seltzer, 1923. Various reprints, including New York: Viking, 1964. Also collected in **321**. P (Viking Compass Book).

"American consciousness has so far been a false dawn. The negative ideal of democracy. But underneath, and contrary to this open ideal, the first hints and revelations of ɪᴛ. ɪᴛ, the American whole soul.

"You have got to pull the democratic and idealistic clothes off American utterance, and see what you can of the dusky body of ɪᴛ underneath. . . .

"The artist usually sets out—or used to—to point a moral and adorn a tale. The tale, however, points the other way, as a rule. Two blankly opposing morals, the artist's and the tale's. Never trust the artist. Trust the tale. The proper function of a critic is to save the tale from the artist who created it."

The iconoclastic, sometimes shrill tone of these intermittently illuminating essays on Franklin, Crèvecoeur, Cooper, Poe, Hawthorne, R. H. Dana, Melville, and Whitman resulted in part from Lawrence's extensive revisions. See Armin Arnold's edition of *The Symbolic Meaning: The Uncollected Versions of Studies in Classic American Literature* (New York: Viking, 1964).

142.   Levin, David. *In Defense of Historical Literature: Essays on American History, Autobiography, Drama, and Fiction*. New York: Hill & Wang, 1967.

"I have spent most of my professional life on the unfortified frontier between university departments of English and history. The region that I have patrolled, however, is not simply the old virgin land of American Studies, so richly

cultivated during the last twenty-five years, but the less
populous territory of historical literature. This book ex-
presses my belief in the value of that literature and my conviction that citizens on both sides of the frontier can learn much
about their own provinces from improved communication
across the border. I propose to illustrate [in essays on Cotton
Mather, Franklin, the Salem witchcraft trials, Hawthorne,
and Faulkner] some of the advantages of examining history
and biography with the eye of a literary critic; fiction and
drama, with an interest in historical theory and fact." See also
Professor Levin's *History as Romantic Art: Bancroft, Prescott,
Motley, and Parkman* (1959).

143.   Levin, Harry. *The Power of Blackness: Hawthorne, Poe, Melville.*
New York: Knopf, 1958. P (Vintage Book).
" 'Following darkness like a dream,' the value of the pursuit
will probably lie in the detailed applications we are able to
make along the way. Our theme will concretely link two broad
assumptions: the symbolic character of our greatest fiction
and the dark character of our deeper minds. Together they
constitute what I would rather describe as an antithesis than
as a thesis, since they act in opposition to more publicized
influences, blandly materialistic."

144.   Lewis, R. W. B. *The American Adam: Innocence, Tragedy, and
Tradition in the Nineteenth Century.* Chicago: University of
Chicago Press, 1955. P (Phoenix Book).
"The American myth saw life and history as just beginning.
It described the world as starting up again under fresh initia-
tive, in a divinely granted second chance for the human race,
after the first chance had been so disastrously fumbled in the
darkening Old World. It introduced a new kind of hero . . .an
individual emancipated from history, happily bereft of ancestry, untouched and undefiled by the usual inheritances of
family and race; an individual standing alone, self-reliant and
self-propelling, ready to confront whatever awaited him with
the aid of his own unique and inherent resources. . . . The
world and history lay all before him. And he was the type of
creator, the poet par excellence, creating language itself by
naming the elements of the scene around him. All this and
more were contained in the image of the American as Adam."

Literary History of the United States (LHUS). See **194.**

145. Litz, A. Walton. *Modern American Fiction: Essays in Criticism.* New York: Oxford University Press, 1963. P (Galaxy Book).

Twenty essays by various hands on Stephen Crane, Dreiser, Gertrude Stein, Sherwood Anderson, Lewis, Fitzgerald, Dos Passos, Faulkner, Hemingway, Wolfe, Steinbeck, and Robert Penn Warren; framed by sections on "Background" and "Foreground."

146. Lynn, Kenneth S. *The Dream of Success: A Study of the Modern American Imagination.* Boston: Little, Brown, 1955.

"In the decade before the Civil War, a new literature began to appear in quantity in the United States. Its forms were various, but it was dedicated to a single theme; life in America was a fluid, wide-open race in which everyone competed on an equal basis—winner take all. . . .

"Alger's first success novel—*Ragged Dick; or Street Life in New York with the Boot-Blacks*—was published in 1868; from that moment, he went on to become the most popular author in American history. . . . The Alger hero fired the American imagination at the instant of his maximum credibility. But when the children born in the year of *Ragged Dick* and after began to come of age in the late eighties and early nineties, they discovered that America's spectacular growth had also spawned a host of problems too big to be ignored. Industrial warfare, political explosions in the farm belt, rising popular bitterness about monopolies and outbursts of xenophobic hatred were simply the most sensational signs of social trouble. . . . The world was, increasingly, out of joint, and as the nineteenth century drew to a close it devolved upon that Hamlet-figure, the American intellectual, to set it right. . . . The trouble was, though, that . . . the five novelists—Dreiser, London, Phillips, Norris, Herrick—who are considered in this study found that to adjust the success myth, on which they had grown up, to the reality which they saw around them was a complex, ambiguous and dramatic task."

147. Martin, Jay. *Harvests of Change: American Literature, 1865-1914.* Englewood Cliffs, N.J.: Prentice-Hall, 1967. P (Spectrum).

"The changes that took place in America between the Civil War and the First World War were remarkable both for their completeness and for their rapidity. Institutions, systems of belief, ideological and social assumptions, ways of feeling at home in the world—in short, the whole scene of human endeavor and thought—that had existed, as Henry Adams said, since the Middle Ages, now passed away during this fifty-year period. . . . Out of the common confusion writers became, as seldom before, public men: they mixed and mingled, sharing their visions with their contemporaries. . . . [They] undertook the task of preserving culture and accommodating change to human uses by clarifying, deepening, and intensifying the contents of consciousness for their age."

148. Martin, Terence. *The Instructed Vision: Scottish Common Sense Philosophy and the Origins of American Fiction.* Bloomington: Indiana University Press, 1961.

"Taught extensively in American colleges and universities, based on metaphysical principles identical with those underlying the prevailing American attitude toward fiction, the philosophy of Common Sense could lend new force to the American suspicion of the imagination at the very time new force was necessary. As we shall see, it offered an enlightened and extremely effective means of controlling the imagination to a society which believed in the need for such control. As a consequence, it contributed to the special problems of the would-be American writer of fiction, for it made fiction more difficult to imagine as an independent, autonomous kind of expression. Yet, as I see it, the implications of Scottish Common Sense thought, suffused into social attitudes, may have pushed the writer who had sufficient audacity toward the creation of the romance, which, by means of its traditional imaginative latitude, could offer him a mode of creative release."

149. Marx, Leo. *The Machine in the Garden: Technology and the Pastoral Ideal in America.* New York: Oxford University Press, 1964. P (Galaxy Book).

"My purpose is to describe and evaluate the uses of the pastoral ideal in the interpretation of American experience. I shall be tracing its adaptation to the conditions of life in the New World, its emergence as a distinctively American theory of society, and its subsequent transformation under the impact of industrialism. . . . This is not, strictly speaking, a book about literature; it is about the region of culture where literature, general ideas, and certain products of the collective imagination—we may call them 'cultural symbols'—meet. To appreciate the significance and power of our American fables it is necessary to understand the interplay between the literary imagination and what happens outside literature, in the general culture. My special concern is to show how the pastoral ideal has been incorporated in a powerful metaphor of contradiction—a way of ordering meaning and value that clarifies our situation today."

150. Matthiessen, F. O. *American Renaissance: Art and Expression in the Age of Emerson and Whitman*. New York: Oxford University Press, 1941. P (Galaxy Book).

The structure of Matthiessen's monumental study of Emerson, Thoreau, Hawthorne, Melville, and Whitman is based on recurrent themes which concern "the adequacy of the different writers' conceptions of the relation of the individual to society, and of the nature of good and evil—these two themes rising to their fullest development in the treatment of tragedy; the stimulus that lay in the transcendental conviction that the word must become one with the thing; the effect produced by the fact that when these writers began their careers, the one branch of literature in which America had a developed tradition was oratory; the effect of the nineteenth century's stress on seeing, of its identification of the poet with the prophet or seer; the connection, real if somewhat intangible, between this emphasis on vision and that put on light by the advancing arts of photography and open-air painting; the inevitability of the symbol as a means of expression for an age that was determined to make a fusion between appearance and what lay behind it; the major desire on the part of all five writers that there should be no split between art and the other functions of the community, that there should be an organic union between labor and culture."

151. Mencken, H. L. *The American Language: An Inquiry into the Development of English in the United States*. 1919; rev. ed., 1921; 3rd ed., 1923; 4th ed., 1936; *Supplement I*, 1945; *Supplement II*, 1948. 4th ed. corrected, enlarged, and rewritten, New York: Knopf, 1965.

Mencken's prodigious labor of almost four decades is still the most substantial and comprehensive treatment of the English language in America. In 1963 Raven I. McDavid, Jr., edited a useful one-volume "abridgement and condensation of Mencken's three volumes, with updating where necessary and editorial commentary at critical points." See **10, 225, 230, 238, 243**, as well as George P. Krapp's *The English Language in*

America (2 vols., 1925), Thomas Pyles's *Words and Ways of American English* (1952), Albert H. Marckwardt's *American English* (1958), and W. N. Francis' *The Structure of American English* (1958).

152.   Merideth, Robert, ed. *American Studies: Essays on Theory and Method*. Columbus, Ohio: Merrill, 1968. P.

"In this first collection of [sixteen] essays devoted entirely to theory and method in American Studies, scholars and students will have available the documents that, especially taken as a whole, begin to give unity to the variety of their enterprise." Cf. **96, 113, 116, 139**.

153.   Miller, Perry. *Errand into the Wilderness*. Cambridge, Mass.: Harvard University Press, 1956. P (Harper Torchbook).

"Omitting, for reasons both of space and policy, works of which I am downright ashamed, along with others that I recast into chapters for either volume of *The New England Mind (The Seventeenth Century*, 1939, 1953; *From Colony to Province*, 1952 [**154**]), I here put together those that seem to add up to a rank of spotlights on the massive narrative of the movement of European culture into the vacant wilderness of America. . . .

"They looked in vain to history for an explanation of themselves; more and more it appeared that the meaning was not to be found in theology, even with the help of the covenantal dialectic. Thereupon, these citizens found that they had no other place to search but within themselves—even though, at first sight, that repository appeared to be nothing but a sink of iniquity. Their errand having failed in the first sense of the term, they were left with the second, and required to fill it with meaning by themselves and out of themselves. Having failed to rivet the eyes of the world upon their city on the hill, they were left alone with America." See next entry.

154.   Miller, Perry. *The New England Mind: The Seventeenth Century*. New York: Macmillan, 1939; reissued 1954. P (Beacon). *The New England Mind: From Colony to Province*. Cambridge, Mass.: Harvard University Press, 1953. P (Beacon).

"If the earlier book [i.e., *The Seventeenth Century*] has any merit it arises from the effort to comprehend, in the widest possible terms, the architecture of the intellect brought to America by the founders of New England. Hence that book was organized by topics, treating the entire expression of the period as a single body of writing and paying little or no attention to modifications forced upon the mind by domestic events. The method could be justified because throughout the century, and down to the first decades of the eighteenth, the official cosmology did remain more or less intact. Such developments as took place affected the lesser areas of church polity, political relations, or the contests of groups and interests. These could be, and indeed as I believe [*From Colony to Province*] demonstrates often were, intense and shattering experiences without causing any alterations in the doctrinal frame of reference. Therefore *From Colony to Province* may be imagined as taking place, so to speak, inside *The Seventeenth Century*. While the massive structure of logic, psychology, theology stands apparently untouched, the furnishings of the palace are little by little changed, until a hundred years after the Great Migration the New England mind has become strangely altered, even though the process (which, all things considered, was rapid) was hardly perceptible to the actors themselves. A hundred years after the landings, they were forced to look upon themselves with amazement, hardly capable of understanding how they had come to be what they were." See the previous entry as well as Professor Miller's *Orthodoxy in Massachusetts* (1933)— "my version of the first two decades of the New England enterprise"—and *The Raven and the Whale: The War of Words and Wits in the Era of Poe and Melville* (1956).

155.   Morgan, H. Wayne, ed. *The Gilded Age*. 1963. Rev. and enl. ed., Syracuse, N.Y.: Syracuse University Press, 1970. P.

  "In the early 1960s the Editor organized a symposium designed to examine critically the historical facts and interpretations available on the period in American history generally known as the Gilded Age. *The Gilded Age: A Reappraisal* appeared in 1963 and has served enough readers to warrant a revised and enlarged edition. The focus remains on the post-Civil War generation. The introductory chapter has been enlarged to cover new material in this edition and establish the theme of nationalization amid industrial change. Essays on genteel reform, the currency question, the Democratic party, populism, the Republican party, and foreign policy were written especially for this edition. The other chapters [on business, labor, civil service reform, literature, science, and popular culture] have been edited, updated, or thoroughly revised."

156. Morison, Samuel Eliot. *The Intellectual Life of Colonial New England*. Ithaca, N.Y.: Cornell University Press, 1956. P. Originally published in 1936 as *The Puritan Pronaos: Studies in the Intellectual Life of New England in the Seventeenth Century*.

"The English puritans who emigrated to New England in the 1630s intended, and in great measure succeeded, in transmitting European civilization to the New World. Realizing that all departments of life not directly useful or absolutely necessary were apt to be sloughed off in a struggle with the wilderness, anticipating that intellectual degeneracy would lead to spiritual decay, they made great sacrifices to transplant the apparatus of civilized life and learning: a university college, grammar schools, elementary schools, printing press, and libraries. . . . Thus, the story of the intellectual life of New England in the seventeenth century . . . is one of the principal approaches to the social and intellectual history of the United States. Primitive New England is a puritan pronaos to the American mind of the nineteenth century, and of today."

Professor Morison's more than forty books include *The European Discovery of America*, in two volumes: *The Northern Voyages, 500-1600* (1971) and *The Southern Voyages, 1492-1616* (1974). See also the next two entries.

157. Morison, Samuel Eliot. *The Oxford History of the American People*. New York: Oxford University Press, 1965. P (New American Library, 2 vols.).

"Politics are not lacking; but my main ambition is to recreate for my readers American ways of living in bygone eras. Here you will find a great deal on social and economic development; horses, ships, popular sports, and pastimes; eating, drinking, and smoking habits. Pugilists will be found cheek-by-jowl with Presidents; rough-necks with reformers, artists with ambassadors."

158. Morison, Samuel Eliot, Henry Steele Commager, and William E. Leuchtenburg. *The Growth of the American Republic*. 2 vols. 6th ed., rev. and enl. New York: Oxford University Press, 1969.

A solid, standard, 1900-page history, written for those "for whom economy in truth-telling is neither necessary nor appropriate. We believe that history embraces the whole of a people's activity: economic and social, literary and spiritual, as well as political and military." For the economy minded, there is a drastically abbreviated *Shorter History of the United States* by Commager and Allan Nevins in the Random House Modern Library series.

159. Mott, Frank Luther. *American Journalism: A History 1690-1960. 1960*. 3rd ed. New York: Macmillan, 1962.

"This is primarily a history of the American newspaper [but] some little attention has been given to the magazines of each period." See **161**.

160. Mott, Frank Luther. *Golden Multitudes: The Story of Best Sellers in the United States*. New York: Macmillan, 1947.

"Popular reading furnishes subject matter for important and fascinating studies. Especially is the thoughtful observer of the workings of a democratic society concerned with the mass impact of so much reading matter upon the public. Only the cynic and the heedless can disregard popular literature. Here the sociologist finds material for his inquiries into the mores, the social historian sees the sign-posts of the development of a people, and students of government observe popular movements at work. As the best sellers are passed in review in the ensuing pages, readers may note their reflection of historical incidents and the development of American society, as well as the reappearance in them of such unifying elements as religion, sensation, self-help, good narration, and so on. After all, *vox populi*, if something less than *vox dei*, is at least a voice to which we must hearken." Cf. **117** and **165**.

161. Mott, Frank Luther. *A History of American Magazines*. 5 vols.: I. *1741-1850*, II. *1850-1865*, III. *1865-1885*, IV. *1885-1905*, V. *1905-1930*. New York: Appleton; Cambridge, Mass.: Harvard University Press, 1930-68.

"The author was at work on Volume V of his projected six-volume work when he died in 1964. . . . Mott's daughter, Mildred Mott Wedel, has prepared this [fifth] volume for publication and provided notes on changes since her father's death." Volume V contains a cumulative index to the five volumes.

162. Mumford, Lewis. *The Golden Day: A Study in American Literature and Culture*. New York: Boni & Liveright, 1926. P (Dover).

"The settlement of the Atlantic seaboard was the culmination of one process, the breakup of medieval culture, and the beginning of another. If the disintegration went farthest in America, the processes of renewal have, at intervals, been most active in the new country; and it is for the beginnings of a genuine culture, rather than for its relentless exploitation of materials, that the American adventure has been significant. To mark the points at which the culture of the Old World broke down, and to discover in what places a new one has arisen are the two poles of the study. Something of value disappeared with the colonization of America. Why did it disappear? Something of value was created. How did that come about? If I do not fully answer these questions, I purpose, at least, to put them a little more sharply, by tracing them to their historic beginnings, and by putting them in their social context. . . . An imaginative New World came to birth during this period [1830-60], a new hemisphere in the geography of the mind. That world was the climax of American experience. What preceded led up to it: what followed, dwindled away from it; and we who think and write to-day are either continuing the first exploration, or we are disheartened, and relapse into some stale formula, or console ourselves with empty gestures of frivolity."

See also Mumford's *Sticks and Stones: A Study of American Architecture and Civilization* (1924; "*The Golden Day*, published two years after *Sticks and Stones*, rounded out the study of American life begun there.") and *The Brown Decades: A Study of the Arts in America, 1865-1895* (1931; "In this book I took occasion to correct . . . a serious omission in both *Sticks and Stones* and *The Golden Day*: a failure to do justice to the creative forces in America after the Civil War.").

163. Murdock, Kenneth B. *Literature and Theology in Colonial New England*. Cambridge, Mass.: Harvard University Press, 1949.

"I have tried . . . to show that, for better or for worse, the Puritans followed a reasoned and mature literary theory, deliberately chosen in preference to others because it seemed to them adapted to the needs of their audience and in harmony with their whole intellectual scheme. Judged comparatively, by a reader whose religious and artistic sympathies are non-Puritan, the results were sometimes good and sometimes bad; but the concern of this book is less with praise or blame,

although neither is excluded, than with an attempt to describe
Puritan literary theory, to show how it worked, and to point
out the relation between the special characteristics of colonial
Puritan literature and those of Puritan thought."

164. Nye, Russel B. *The Cultural Life of the New Nation, 1776-1830*.
Introd. Henry Steele Commager and Richard B. Morris. New
York: Harper, 1960. P (Harper Torchbook).

"The Revolutionary War powerfully activated the spirit of
nationalism, and that burgeoning nationalism left its imprint
on all our political and cultural institutions. It spawned a
native, indigenous literature and art, a group of American
churches independent of control from abroad, a special edu-
cational [and scientific] approach and system, new and original concepts of constitutional law and government, and a
search for a usable past, for memorials, annals, and heroes so
central to any national tradition."

165. Nye, Russel B. *The Unembarrassed Muse: The Popular Arts in
America*. New York: Dial Press, 1970.

A study of those arts which "express the taste and understanding of the majority and which are free of control, in
content and execution, from minority standards of correct-
ness." There are chapters on fiction, poetry, theater, music,
movies, radio, and television, as well as special studies of the
dime novel, the comics, and of "Cops, Spacemen, and Cow-
boys." Indexed, with a selected bibliography. Cf. **117** and **160**.

166. Olderman, Raymond M. *Beyond the Waste Land: The American
Novel in the Nineteen-Sixties*. New Haven: Yale University
Press, 1973. P.

Discussions of Kesey, Elkin, Barth, Heller, Pynchon,
Hawkes, Vonnegut, Beagle (but not Bellow, Mailer,
Malamud, Percy, Updike)—writers, according to Olderman,
confronted with "a growing sense of the mystery of
fact . . . and a loss of confidence in our own power to effect
change and to control events" who finally affirm "the small
but valuable sense that life is simply better than death."

167. Parrington, Vernon Louis. *Main Currents in American Thought*.
3 vols.: *The Colonial Mind, 1620-1800; The Romantic Revolution
in America, 1800-1860; The Beginnings of Critical Realism,
1860-1920*. New York: Harcourt, Brace, 1927-30. P.

"I have undertaken to give some account of the genesis and

development in American letters of certain germinal ideas that have come to be reckoned traditionally American—how they came into being here, how they were opposed, and what influence they have exerted in determining the form and scope of our characteristic ideals and institutions. In pursuing such a task, I have chosen to follow the broad path of our political, economic, and social development, rather than the narrower belletristic; and the main divisions of the study have been fixed by forces that are anterior to literary schools and movements, creating the body of ideas from which literary culture eventually springs.

"The point of view from which I have endeavored to evaluate the materials is liberal rather than conservative, Jeffersonian rather than Federalistic; and very likely in my search I have found what I went forth to find."

The last volume was left incomplete at Parrington's death in 1929 and published posthumously in fragmentary form.

168. Pattee, Fred Lewis. *A History of American Literature since 1870.* New York: Century, 1915. *The Development of the American Short Story: An Historical Survey.* New York: Harper, 1923. *The New American Literature, 1890-1930.* New York: Century, 1930. *The First Century of American Literature, 1770-1870.* New York: Appleton, Century, 1935.

One of the earliest explorers of American literary history, Pattee intended that these four volumes should be gathered as *A Literary History of the American People*: "My fundamental conception has been that American literature during its century and a half of existence has been an emanation from American life and American conditions. But I have begun in every case with the literary product rather than the historical background, my eye always on the American *people*. . . . I have watched for evolutions from peculiarly American conditions: the evolution of American humor, the American essay, the American newspaper, the American newspaper column, the American short story."

169. Pearce, Roy Harvey. *The Continuity of American Poetry.* Princeton, N.J.: Princeton University Press, 1961. P.

"In short, the power of American poetry from the beginning has derived from the poet's inability, or refusal, at some depth of consciousness wholly to accept his culture's system of values. By the nineteenth century that refusal, freed from its matrix in Puritan dogma, had been in effect transformed into its opposite, a mode of assent; and the American poet again and again imaged himself—in Emerson's and Whitman's word—as an Adam who, since he might well be one with God, was certainly one with all men. The continuity of this narrative is that of the antinominian, Adamic impulse, as it thrusts against a culture made by Americans who come more and more to be frightened by it, even as they realize that it is basic to the very idea of their society: one (in Whitman's words) of simple, separate persons, yet democratic, en-masse.'"

170. Pearce, Roy Harvey. *Savagism and Civilization: A Study of the Indian and the American Mind*. Baltimore: Johns Hopkins Press, 1965. P. Originally published in 1953 as *The Savages of America: A Study of the Indian and the Idea of Civilization*.

"The double image of the Indian, noble and ignoble, had by the end of the first quarter of the [nineteenth] century, been firmly resolved into one image, that of the savage whose life was to be comprehended by the idea of savagism.... His life could not be said to be one totally superior or totally inferior to that of a civilized man. It did not make sense to view his state as one either to be aspired to or to be dismissed with unfeeling contempt; rather it was to be seen as the state of one almost entirely out of contact, for good and for bad, with the life of civilized men. Indian nobility and ignobility, Indian virtues and vices, had to be at once admitted and praised and dispraised for what they were, qualities tied together and delimited by the special nature of Indian society. That society was found as a whole to be morally inferior to civilized society.... The historical fact surely is that our civilization, in subduing the Indian, killed its own creature, the savage."

171. Peden, William. *The American Short Story: Front Line in the National Defense of Literature*. Boston: Houghton Mifflin, 1964.

"Paradox has characterized the development of the short story in America. Although it is the only major literary form of essentially American origin and the only one in which American writers have always tended to excel, it has for decades been considered a parvenu, and until very recently most critics have refused to consider it as important as the more traditional forms of poetry, drama, and the novel...

"The short story in America has always been a thing of individuality, freedom, and variety. Flexibility is its hallmark, and no other literary form is so close to the rapidly changing pulse of the times in which it is written: 'In a nervous and reckless age [according to V. S. Pritchett] which is overwhelmed by enormous experience, we have inevitably formed the habit of seeing . . . in fragments rather than as a solid mass . . . and, because of this, the brief, quickly moving, epigrammatic, allusive habit of the short story usually seems to me a more natural form for our story-telling than the novel. . . .' The short story writer is creating the dominant and characteristic literary form of the post-World War II years."

See **168** for an early history of the short story; and Arthur Voss, *The American Short Story: A Critical Survey* (1973), for the most recent discussion.

172.   Perkins, George, ed. *The Theory of the American Novel*. New York: Holt, Rinehart and Winston, 1970. P.

Critical writings by thirty major American writers.

173.   Petter, Henri. *The Early American Novel*. Columbus: Ohio State University Press, 1971.

"A descriptive and critical survey of the American novel up to the year 1820" by a Swiss scholar who frankly admits that "most of the early American novels are failures." Petter includes synopses of eighty-two novels and a substantial bibliography.

174.   Pizer, Donald. *Realism and Naturalism in Nineteenth-Century American Literature*. Carbondale: Southern Illinois University Press, 1966.

"The realistic or naturalistic novel is thus not a detached and objective account of the destruction of the individual by material force. Nor are these novels composed of slabs of the commonplace and trivial in experience. Beginning with Twain and James, and continuing more strongly and fully in Norris, Crane, and Dreiser, the novelist depicts life as extraordinary and sensational rather than as placid and commonplace. The first generation of late nineteenth-century novelists dramatized the validity of older faiths in areas of contemporary and local experience recently legitimatized for fictional representation. The increasingly profound involvement of the second generation of novelists in all ranges of life led them to that combination of violent action and degrading detail organized around implicit but oblique systems of value which constitutes the modern tragic vision. Thus, late nineteenth-century fiction is not a long and dull hiatus between the romances of Hawthorne and Melville and those of Faulkner, as much current criticism of American fiction implies. It rather moves toward and eventually embodies the intermingling of the commonplace and the sensational, and of the humanly ennobling and the humanly degrading, which characterizes much of contemporary American fiction. . . . The large effect of these studies should be to encourage the view that the literature of late nineteenth-century America is not so simple as it sometimes appears to be."

175. Poirier, Richard. *A World Elsewhere: The Place of Style in American Literature*. New York: Oxford University Press, 1966. P (Galaxy Book).

"That the New World offered architectural opportunities on a scale never equaled before or since scarcely needs repeating, any more than does the explanation that American writers have therefore been addicted to metaphors of 'building' and to theories about the proper housing for expanded states of consciousness. . . . My emphasis in this book will be on the dialectical struggle which this concept has engendered within American writing from Emerson and Cooper to the present. As a conscious play of ideas within works or among writers, this struggle is almost platitudinously obvious and usually defined as part of the fight for literary as well as political independence of Europe. I have tried instead to locate the phenomenon in style, in the rhythms and sounds of sentences, where it has an energy the more intense because of the writer's usually unprogrammatic involvement with the only materials—language—with which he can try to 'build' a world. . . . The style of the most exciting American books is not one of consensus or amelioration among its given constituents, but a style filled with an agitated desire to make a world in which tensions and polarities are fully developed and then resolved."

Among Professor Poirier's other books is a collection of essays on Joyce, Eliot, Frost, Mailer, Pynchon, "The War against the Young," "Learning from the Beatles," and "The Literature of Waste" entitled *The Performing Self: Compositions and Decompositions in the Languages of Contemporary Life* (1971).

176. Porte, Joel. *The Romance in America: Studies in Cooper, Poe, Hawthorne, Melville, and James*. Middletown, Conn.: Wesleyan University Press, 1969. P.

"I have attempted to show that all these writers created, partially or completely, according to a theory of stylized art—heavily dependent on the use of conventional, or archetypal figures and on symbol, parable, dream, and fantasy—in order to explore large questions...about race, history, nature, human motivation, and art. Particularly from Poe to James, I have tried to suggest that the American romance is characterized by a need self-consciously to define its own aims, so that 'romance' becomes frequently ... the theme as well as the form of these authors' works."

177. Quinn, Arthur Hobson. *A History of the American Drama, from the Beginning to the Civil War*. New York: Harper, 1923.

An uncritical but factually useful survey beginning with the first play written by an American and produced professionally, Thomas Godfrey's blank-verse tragedy *The Prince of Parthia*, produced in Philadelphia in 1767. The study is continued in *A History of the American Drama, from the Civil War to the Present Day* (1927; rev. ed., New York: F. S. Crofts, 1936).

178. Quinn, Arthur Hobson, et al. *The Literature of the American People: An Historical and Critical Survey*. New York: Appleton-Century-Crofts, 1951.

Part I: "The Colonial and Revolutionary Period" (Kenneth B. Murdock); Part II: "Establishment of a National Culture" (A. H. Quinn); Part III: "The Later Nineteenth Century" (Clarence Gohdes); Part IV: "The Twentieth Century" (George F. Whicher). Largely superseded by *Literary History of the United States* (**194**).

179. Rahv, Philip. *Image and Idea: Twenty Essays on Literary Themes*. 1949. Rev. and enl. ed., Norfolk, Conn.: James Laughlin, 1957.

Essays, many of which first appeared in *Partisan Review* (Rahv was a founder and editor), on James, Hawthorne, Melville, Hemingway, Eliot; as well as "Paleface and Redskin," "The Cult of Experience in American Writing," "Notes on the Decline of Naturalism," and "American Intellectuals in the Postwar Situation."

"It is perhaps worth noting that the two essays on James were written before the revival of this classic American novelist, a revival long in preparation, which was finally brought to a head, in the fall of 1944, by the simultaneous appearance of two anthologies of his fiction. . . . But it may well be that his apotheosis is not quite what was wanted. For it seems that the long-standing prejudice against him has now given way to an uncritical adulation which, in a different way, is perhaps quite as retarding to a sound appraisal of his achievement."

180. Rideout, Walter B. *The Radical Novel in the United States, 1900-1954: Some Interrelations of Literature and Society*. Cambridge, Mass.: Harvard University Press, 1956. P (Hill & Wang).

"In the following pages I have attempted to conduct neither an attack nor a defense, but rather an examination, as objective an examination as possible, of a body of fiction which once was exaltedly praised in some quarters and now in most quarters is categorically condemned. . . . We still know very little about the obscure and enormously complicated relation between a society and its literature. This study is offered as an attempt to increase at least slightly our knowledge of that relation." Cf. **120**.

181. Rosenthal, M. L. *The Modern Poets: A Critical Introduction*. New York: Oxford University Press, 1960. P(Galaxy Book).

"Without offering an exhaustive survey of *all* the modern poets and poetic currents, I have tried to plot a view that will suggest the range of our poetic landscape and its relation to that crisis of personality the modern mind has had to face for more than a century. The book therefore begins with some comment on the resistance to rapport between poet and reader, on the character of the poetic sensibility revealed to us by the moderns, and on the many and varied continuities between poetry of the past and that of our own time. It then turns to the great germinative figures of Yeats, Pound, and Eliot—all of them extremely sensitive to the rôle of tradition—and to other important figures among the older moderns [including Robinson, Frost, Williams, Stevens, Marianne Moore, Cummings, Sandburg, and Jeffers]. It concludes with chapters on the prophetic, visionary, and rhetorical writing of Lawrence, Crane, and the 'thirties and on the poetry that has risen to the fore in the past two decades, from Dylan Thomas on [including Lowell]."

182.   Rosenthal, M. L. *The New Poets: American and British Poetry since World War II*. New York: Oxford University Press, 1967. P(Galaxy Book).

"The 'new poets' who since World War II have emerged in the United States and the British Isles have done so without apologies to their elders, if not without tutelage from them. The new writing is a real presence. It speaks for certain further turns in the sensibility of this age of drastic, candid confrontations. My aim has been to identify a number of the crucial figures [including Robert Lowell, Sylvia Plath, Allen Ginsberg, Theodore Roethke, John Berryman, Anne Sexton, Denise Levertov, Paul Blackburn, LeRoi Jones, and the Black Mountain group—Robert Creeley, Charles Olson, and Robert Duncan] and poems and to suggest certain meaningful relationships among them in the light of the whole modern tradition."

183.   Rourke, Constance. *American Humor: A Study of the National Character*. New York: Harcourt, Brace, 1931. P(Harvest Book).

A survey of American humor from the pre-Revolutionary period into the twentieth century. "There is scarcely an aspect of the American character to which humor is not related, few which in some sense it has not governed. It has moved into literature not merely as an occasional touch but as a force determining large patterns and intentions." Indexed. See next entry.

184.   Rourke, Constance. *The Roots of American Culture and Other Essays*. Ed., with a preface, Van Wyck Brooks. New York: Harcourt, Brace & World, 1942. P (Harvest Book).

Includes the title essay and others on the rise of theatricals in America, early American music, the Shakers, Negro literature, and the future of American art, gleaned by Brooks from the manuscripts and notes for a "History of American Culture," planned for three volumes, that Miss Rourke left unfinished when she died in 1941. In this and such other works as *Trumpets of Jubilee* (1927), *Troupers of the Gold Coast* (1928), *American Humor* (1931; **183**), *Davy Crockett* (1934), *Audubon* (1936) and *Charles Sheeler* (1938); Constance Rourke opposed the idea that American culture was formed through the "transit of [European] civilization," that Americans were the victims of a "cultural lag": "Was it not rather the case that we had a long folk-life behind us which has found inevitable expression in forms of its own? Had not the critics ignored the creative forces that have always existed in this country? And could these not be shown to constitute an esthetic tradition?"

185. Rubin, Louis D., Jr., ed. *The Comic Imagination in American Literature*. New Brunswick, N.J.: Rutgers University Press, 1973.

The volume consists of thirty-two introductory essays, originally prepared to be broadcast in the Voice of America "Forum" series. "The objective was to sketch out the modes of American comedy, ranging from the journalistic and the subliterary on through the reaches of artistic achievement, to cover some of the leading practitioners of comedy [Franklin, Irving, Holmes, Mark Twain, Henry James, Ambrose Bierce, Mencken, Ring Lardner, Sinclair Lewis, Cabell, Barth, Caldwell, Faulkner, Eudora Welty, Flannery O'Connor, Walker Percy, and others], and to try to suggest some of the relationships between the comic writings of Americans and the problems—literary, philosophical, social, political, economic—of the society whose life they sought to interpret."

186. Rubin, Louis D., Jr. *The Faraway Country: Writers of the Modern South*. Seattle: University of Washington Press, 1963. P (as *Writers of the Modern South*).

The image in the title is from Mark Twain's description of Cardiff Hill in *The Adventures of Tom Sawyer*—"just far away enough to seem a Delectable Land, dreamy, reposeful, and inviting."

"To understand the literature of the South of our own time, it is essential to keep in mind the small-town, small-city origins of the writers who created it. They grew up at a time when the fabric of Southern community life as it had existed for many decades was beginning to break up before the forces of the twentieth century. As writers they are themselves symbols, I think, of that disintegration."

Modern Southern writers "live in another country. It is not the country in which they were born, nor the country to which they once fled, nor yet the South to which they came back. Like Mark Twain's Mississippi River community, it is the country of fiction. There they may see the meaning of things in time, for as they write they step outside of everyday life toward a timeless perspective in which a fountain splashing in the town square becomes a sign of change, a Confederate cemetery a symbol of man caught in time, a rotting mansion in the Mississippi wilderness the emblem of what human beings in a time and place aspired to be, and what they became."

Includes essays on George W. Cable, Faulkner, Thomas Wolfe, Robert Penn Warren, Eudora Welty, Donald Davidson, John Crowe Ransom, Allen Tate, and William Styron.

Among Rubin's other studies of Southern literature are *The Writer in the South: Studies in a Literary Community* (1972); *Southern Renascence: The Literature of the Modern South*, essays edited with Robert D. Jacobs (1953, rpt. 1966; P); and *South: Modern Southern Literature in Its Cultural Setting*, a collection of essays edited with Robert D. Jacobs (1961).

187.   Schneider, Herbert W. *A History of American Philosophy*. 1946. 2nd ed., New York: Columbia University Press, 1963. P.

"The reader of the story that follows will note that American philosophy has continually been given new life and new directions by waves of immigration. In America, at least, it is useless to seek a 'native' tradition, for even our most genteel traditions are saturated with foreign inspirations. Spanish Franciscans, French Jesuits, English Puritans, Dutch Pietists, Scottish Calvinists, cosmopolitan *philosophes*, German Transcendentalists, Russian revolutionaries, and Oriental theosophists have all shared in giving to so-called American philosophy its continuities as well as its shocks. The extent to which American intellectual life has been dependent on non-American scholars is incommensurate with the extent to which American philosophers have enjoyed influence abroad. Emerson himself, with all his independence, was certainly not made in America alone; he absorbed from Europe and Asia much more than he gave them. America was intellectually colonial long after it gained political independence and has been intellectually provincial long after it ceased being intellectually colonial. We still live intellectually on the fringe of European culture."

188.   Shea, Daniel B., Jr. *Spiritual Autobiography in Early America*. Princeton, N.J.: Princeton University Press, 1968.

"In place of inclusive historical description, I have sought instead to locate the principle by which a given autobiographer selected from the details of his experience and according to which he shaped the narrative which was finally allowed to stand as the image of his soul. . . . A Puritan sought to assemble the evidence for divine favoritism toward him, and many Quaker journals recount the protracted search of the narrator for Truth, which he inevitably finds in the doctrines of the Society of Friends. But conventions are always more apparent from a distance, and by getting close to individual narratives I hope to show that the argument of early American autobiography is considerably more various than scholars have assumed, and fraught with more difficulties than its avowed didactic purpose would suggest."

Includes a bibliographical essay.

189. Smith, Bernard. *Forces in American Criticism: A Study in the History of American Literary Thought*. New York: Harcourt, Brace, 1939.

"I became interested in finding out to what degree one could relate the history of American literature to the history of American life. It occurred to me that the real link in that relationship is the attitude toward literature that men have had under varying circumstances—the ideas they have had regarding its value and purpose and the way its excellence or lack of it may be determined. In other words, literary criticism seemed to me more clearly related to social history than are poetry and fiction."

190. Smith, Henry Nash. *Virgin Land: The American West as Symbol and Myth*. Cambridge, Mass.: Harvard University Press, 1950. Reissued, with a new preface, 1970. P.

A classic and trend-setting work in American studies which "traces the impact of the West, the vacant continent beyond the frontier, on the consciousness of Americans and follows the principal consequences of this impact in literature and social thought down to Turner's formulation of it [in 1893]. . . .

"The early visions of an American Empire embody two different if often mingled conceptions. There is on the one hand the notion of empire as command of the sea, and on the other hand the notion of empire as a populous future society occupying the interior of the American continent. . . . Both these conceptions predict the outcome of the westward movement. Empire conceived as maritime dominion presupposes American expansion westward to the Pacific. The idea draws upon the long history and rich overtones of the search

for a northwest passage to Asia, or, in Whitman's phrase, a
'passage to India.' It will occupy our attention in Book One.
The hunter and trapper who served as the pathfinder of
overland expansion and became one of the fixtures of American mythology forms the subject of Book Two. The very
different idea of a continental empire dependent upon ag-
riculture, and associated with various images of the Good
Society to be realized in the West, may be called the theme of
the Garden of the World. Its development will be traced in
Book Three."

191. Spencer, Benjamin T. *The Quest for Nationality*. Syracuse,
      N.Y.: Syracuse University Press, 1957.
          "This book is a history of the attempt of American authors,
      critics and patriots to design and foster a national literature
      during the three centuries after the first settlement. Based as
      it is on explicit critical comment it is concerned rather with
      literary intention than result." The history stops in 1892, after
      the deaths of Whitman, Lowell, and Melville. It includes an
      extensive bibliography of critical sources.

192. Spiller, Robert E. *The Cycle of American Literature: An Essay in
      Historical Criticism*. New York: Macmillan, 1955. P (Free
      Press).
          This work is "inescapably a by-product of the shared ex-
      perience of editing the *Literary History of the United States*
      [**194**]. . . . The American expansion to the West, and the im-
      pact in turn of the newly formed civilization on its parent, set
      the circular pattern for the whole story. . . . When applied to
      the story of American literature as a whole, this cyclic theory
      discloses not only a single organic movement, but at least two
      secondary cycles as well: the literary movement which de-
      veloped from the Eastern seaboard as a center, and culmi-
      nated with the great romantic writers of the mid-nineteenth
      century; and that which grew out of the conquest of the
      continent and is now rounding its full cycle in the twentieth
      century."

193. Spiller, Robert E., ed. *A Time of Harvest: American Literature,
      1910-1960*. New York: Hill & Wang, 1962. P.
          "A series of [fifteen] connected and developing historical
      essays [by different scholars] arranged in a more or less logical
      and chronological order" based on a "high degree of consen-
      sus among American literary historians today" that did not

exist "in the 1940's when a similar historical interpretation was set up, somewhat provisionally, as the structural frame of the *Literary History of the United States* [**194**]." That consensus, according to Spiller, affirms the "existence and general character of a second literary renaissance in the United States between 1910 and 1940 . . . [which] saw the rise, the flowering, and the decline of naturalism in American literature, accompanied by a vigorous critical movement which gave it control and direction."

194.   Spiller, Robert E., et al. *Literary History of the United States: History.* 1948. 4th ed., rev., New York: Macmillan, 1974.

"Each generation should produce at least one literary history of the United States, for each generation must define the past in its own terms. A redefinition of our literary past was needed at the time of the First World War, when the *Cambridge History of American Literature* [**92**] was produced by a group of scholars. It is now needed again. . . . The United States, in its life of less than two centuries, has produced too much literature for any one man to read and digest. Its literary history can therefore be best written by a group of collaborators, whatever the risk of differences of perspective and opinion."

LHUS consisted originally of eighty-one essays (on major authors, topics, and cultural backgrounds) by fifty-six collaborators (e.g., Blackmur, Canby, Cowley, H. M. Jones, Krutch, Matthiessen, Murdock, H. N. Smith, Spiller, Stegner, Thorp, Van Doren, Wecter) who at mid-century constituted the pantheon of American literary scholarship. The original two volumes (Vol. III was a bibliography) were combined in a single-volume "revised edition" in 1953. A decade later two chapters were added to this revised edition and it was reprinted as *Literary History of the United States: History*, 3rd ed. In the fourth edition "the editors have resisted the temptation to alter the main text; but new scholarship has made imperative, and the coming of a new editor has made possible, a wholly new chapter on Emily Dickinson. The chapter on the 'End of an Era,' dealing with the writers who survived World War II, has also been virtually rewritten as time has cleared perspective; the 'Postscript' section has been dropped and new chapters by Ihab Hassan, Daniel Hoffman, and Gerald Weales have brought the *History* into the new generation."

See **58** for the companion *Literary History of the United States: Bibliography*.

195.   Stovall, Floyd, ed. *The Development of American Literary Criticism*. Chapel Hill: University of North Carolina Press, 1955. P (College and University Press of New Haven).

"Although the lines of development are obscure, it is apparent to one who will follow them closely that American criticism, like American literature, has a strong native element, and that its growth has been to a great extent independent of European models of the same period. There have been and continue to be internal tensions, conflicting tendencies, but these are not finally disintegrating; rather they are the means and the evidence of organic growth. During the first century of American national independence this growth was, in general, away from the European tradition and towards the establishment of a cognate but independent American tradition. Once such a tradition was established our nationalism lost its aggressiveness, and since the begining of the present century the lines of development of American and European criticism have converged and now follow approximately parallel directions. This is not a denial of the continuing existence of a national American criticism but a proof that it has reached maturity. We can at last, as we could not in Emerson's time without arrogance, stand on our own feet."

The volume consists of five essays: "Changing Attitudes in Early American Literary Criticism, 1800-1840" (H. H. Clark); "Organic Form in American Criticism, 1840-1870" (R. H. Fogle); "The Literary Criticism of the Genteel Decades, 1870-1900" (R. P. Falk); "Revolt and Revaluation in Criticism, 1900-1930" (J. H. Raleigh); "The Defense of Art: Criticism since 1930" (C. H. Holman).

196.   Straumann, Heinrich. *American Literature in the Twentieth Century*. 1951. 3rd ed., rev., New York: Harper & Row, 1968. P (Harper & Row Perennial Library edition).

An attempt, by a European, to write "not a history of American literature ... but a study in attitudes [which describes] the basic conceptions of life underlying the works of some of the outstanding writers of the century, and the values they believe in. Above all, it tries to establish the links between what novelists, dramatists and poets have expressed, and the views of some essayists and especially of the leading philosophers who, in fact, provide the natural framework of the whole. It starts from the assumption that, however different the various trends of thought and means of expression, an age has a definite character. It undertakes to analyse its main aspects with a view to arriving at an understanding of the apparent contradictions and puzzling complexities of the modern American outlook."

197. Tanner, Tony. *City of Words: American Fiction, 1950-1970*. New York: Harper & Row, 1971.
A study of twenty-five American novelists since 1950 which discusses, among other things, "the problematical and ambiguous relationship of the self to patterns of all kinds—social, psychological, linguistic—[which] is an obsession among recent American writers. . . . It is my contention that many recent American writers are unusually aware of this quite fundamental and inescapable paradox: that to exist, a book, a vision, a system, like a person, has to have an outline—there can be no identity without contour. But contours signify arrest, they involve restraint and the acceptance of limits."

198. Tanner, Tony. *The Reign of Wonder: Naivety and Reality in American Literature*. Cambridge, Eng.: Cambridge University Press, 1965.
"A major problem facing American writers was simply, overwhelmingly, the need to recognize and contain a new continent. The wondering vision was adopted as a prime method of inclusion and assimilation. [Furthermore,] the stance of wonder has *remained* a preferred way of dealing with experience and confronting existence among American writers. With these two considerations in mind it seems to me legitimate to study the recurring use of wonder and the naive vision in American literature as something related, indeed, to a general European phenomenon, but more importantly as a phenomenon unique in itself. This is not to stress the 'American-ness' of American literature but only to suggest that certain problems and certain solutions are observably present in many American writers and that these may be profitably approached by considering their predilection for the strategy of the naive vision, that deliberate attempt to regard reality with minimum reference to previous familiar-

ity and interpretative knowledge, that enduring preference for wonder over analysis.

"This book attempts to show that many American writers [especially Emerson, Thoreau, Whitman, Mark Twain, Henry James, Gertrude Stein, Sherwood Anderson, and Hemingway] worked to develop a new point of view, a new way of appropriating reality, a new angle of vision [which incorporates] three basic interests: the interest in the naive eye with its unselective wonder; the interest in the vernacular with its immediacy and concrete directness; and the effort to slough off the Past and concentrate exclusively on the present moment."

199. Taylor, Walter Fuller. *The Economic Novel in America*. Chapel Hill: University of North Carolina Press, 1942.

"In the following pages, my aim has been to describe and interpret the response given by American authorship to one of the major social forces of the latter nineteenth century— the rapid industrialization of our American society, the sudden maturation of the Machine Age. More specifically, I have proposed to show how, between the Civil War and the turn of the century, certain democratic and middle-class ideals, which had hitherto been applied chiefly to politics, were so extended as to apply to economics as well; how that democratic ideology found voice in our published fiction [especially that of Mark Twain, Garland, Bellamy, Howells, and Norris]; and how, consequently, there developed within that fiction a coherent and incisive *critique* of capitalistic industrialism.

"During my examination of this body of critical literature, I have been led, by the clear indications of historical evidence, into strenuous disagreement with certain widely held ideas about the complacency and cultural enervation of the so-called Gilded Age; so that the general drift of my work is toward the rehabilitation of that somewhat maligned era."

200. Thorp, Willard. *American Writing in the Twentieth Century*. Cambridge, Mass.: Harvard University Press, 1960.

"In Chapter One ('The Age of Innocence') the chief stress is on the novels of the period from 1900 to 1914 since little poetry or drama of importance was written during those years. The second chapter ('New Voices') describes the renaissance in poetry and fiction which took place between 1912 and 1922. The subject of Chapter Three will be clear at once from the title: 'Dramatic Interlude, 1915-1940.' Two chapters are then devoted to the many novelists of distinction who began to publish after the First World War. To give these chapters coherence and shape they are organized thematically: Chapter Four being called 'Caste and Class in the Novel, 1920-1950' and Chapter Five, 'The Persistence of Naturalism in the Novel.' In each of these chapters there is a backward glance to the earlier years of the century. Chapter Six, 'Make It New: Poetry, 1920-1950,' parallels these two chapters on the novelists.

"During this half-century span there were several regional movements in our literature. Of these the most influential and long-lived was the 'Southern Renaissance,' which is the subject of Chapter Seven. Because throughout this period critical writing kept pace with the work of the novelists, poets, and dramatists, it seemed appropriate to devote the concluding chapter ('Off to the Critical Wars') to the critics who praised or dissented from, but in any event analyzed and debated, the new writing season by season. I have concluded each chapter with a several-page consideration of at least one outstanding writer whose work is representative of the period or theme under discussion. It has thus been possible to introduce critical surveys of the work of Edith Wharton, E. A. Robinson, Robert Frost, Willa Cather, Eugene O'Neill, John Dos Passos, Ernest Hemingway, Wallace Stevens, William Faulkner, and T. S. Eliot."

201. Tocqueville, Alexis de. *Democracy in America*. 2 vols. 1835-40. P (Vintage: the Henry Reeve translation as revised by Francis Bowen, ed. Phillips Bradley; Doubleday Anchor: trans. George Lawrence from 2nd rev. and corrected text of the 1961 French edition, ed. J. P. Mayer).

Alexis-Charles-Henri-Maurice Clérel, comte de Tocqueville, was sent to the United States in 1831 by the French government to report on the American prison system. Upon returning to France he published in four volumes the first comprehensive study of the political and social conditions, attitudes, and institutions in the United States.

"Among the novel objects that attracted my attention during my stay in the United States, nothing struck me more forcibly than the general equality of condition among the people. I readily discovered the prodigious influence that this primary fact exercises on the whole course of society; it gives a peculiar direction to public opinion and a peculiar tenor to the laws; it imparts new maxims to the governing authorities and peculiar habits to the governed.

"I soon perceived that the influence of this fact extends far beyond the political character and the laws of the country, and that it has no less effect on civil society than on the government; it creates opinions, gives birth to new sentiments, founds novel customs, and modifies whatever it does not produce. The more I advanced in the study of American society, the more I perceived that this equality of condition is the fundamental fact from which all others seem to be derived and the central point at which all my observations constantly terminated."

202. Trilling, Lionel. *The Liberal Imagination: Essays on Literature and Society.* New York: Viking, 1950. P(Compass Book).

Sixteen distinguished essays, including "Reality in America," "Freud and Literature," and "Manners, Morals, and the Novel," as well as discussions of Sherwood Anderson, Mark Twain, Fitzgerald, and Henry James.

"In the United States at this time liberalism is not only the dominant but even the sole intellectual tradition. . . . It is one of the tendencies of liberalism to simplify, and this tendency is natural in view of the effort which liberalism makes to organize the elements of life in a rational way. . . . Organization means delegation, and agencies, and bureaus, and technicians, and that the ideas that can survive delegation, that can be passed on to agencies and bureaus and technicians, incline to be ideas of a certain simplicity: they give up something of their largeness and modulation and complexity in order to survive. . . . The job of criticism would seem to be, then, to recall liberalism to its first essential imagination of variousness and possibility, which implies the awareness of complexity and difficulty. To the carrying out of the job of criticizing the liberal imagination, literature has a unique relevance, not merely because so much of modern literature has explicitly directed itself upon politics, but more importantly because literature is the human activity that takes the fullest and most precise account of variousness, possibility, complexity, and difficulty."

Professor Trilling's other books include *The Opposing Self: Nine Essays in Criticism* (1955) and *Beyond Culture* (1965).

203. Tuttleton, James W. *The Novel of Manners in America*. Chapel
Hill: University of North Carolina Press, 1972. P (Norton).

This book is in many ways a reply to Lionel Trilling ("The
novel in America diverges from its classic intention, which, as
I have said, is the investigation of the problem of reality
beginning in the social field. The fact is that American writers
of genius have not turned their minds to society"; see "Manners, Morals, and the Novel," collected in **202**) and Richard
Chase ("The novelist needs a more vivid variety of manners
than, so far, he has discovered in this country"; see *The American Novel and Its Tradition* [**94**]).

Professor Tuttleton argues that "America as a nation is
marked by a significant cultural diversity" and that "the novel
of manners itself deserves higher esteem than recent
critics—particularly those ideologically committed to avant-
garde experimentalism in literature and to radicalism in
politics—have accorded it." Defining the novel of manners as
one in which "the manners, social customs, folkways, conventions, traditions, and mores of a given social group at a given
time and place play a dominant role in the lives of fictional
characters," he seeks "to elucidate its typical themes, styles,
structures, character types, ideological postures, and the
characteristic strategies by which the form is brought to life by
our novelists [Cooper, James, Howells, Wharton, Lewis,
Fitzgerald, O'Hara, Marquand, Cozzens, and Auchincloss]."

204. Tyler, Moses Coit. *A History of American Literature*. 2 vols.: I:
1607-1676; II: *1676-1765*. New York: Putnam, 1878. Rpt.
Ithaca, N.Y.: Cornell University Press, 1949.

"The present volumes . . . may be described as a history of
the rise of American literature at the several isolated colonial
centres, where at first each had its peculiar literary accent; of
the growth of this sporadic colonial literature in copiousness,
range, flexibility, in elegance and force, and especially in
tendency toward a common national accent; until, finally, in
1765, after all the years of our minority and of our filial
obedience had been lived, the scattered voices of the thirteen
colonies were for the first time brought together and blended
in one great and resolute utterance—an utterance expressive
of criticism upon the parental control wielded over us by
England, of dissent from that control, and at last of resistance
to it." See next entry.

205. Tyler, Moses Coit. *The Literary History of the American Revolution, 1763-1783*. 2 vols. New York: Putnam's, 1897. Rpt. New York: Barnes and Noble, 1941; New York: Ungar, 1957.

"The chief trait, therefore, of American literature during the period now under view is this: its concern with the problems of American society, and of American society in a peculiar condition—aroused, inflammable, in a state of alarm for its own existence, but also in a state of resolute combat for it. The literature which we are thus to inspect is not, then, a literature of tranquillity, but chiefly a literature of strife, or, as the Greeks would have said, of agony; and, of course, it must take those forms in which intellectual and impassioned debate can be most effectually carried on. The literature of our Revolution has almost everywhere the combative note; its habitual method is argumentative, persuasive, appealing, rasping, retaliatory; the very brain of man seems to be in armor; his wit is in the gladiator's attitude of offense and defense. It is a literature indulging itself in grimaces, in mockery, in scowls: a literature accented by earnest gestures meant to convince people, or by fierce blows meant to smite them down. In this literature we must not expect to find art used for art's sake. Nay, art itself, so far as it is here at all, is swept into the universal conscription, and enrolled for the service of the one party or of the other in the imperilled young Republic. No man is likely to be in the mood for aesthetics who has an assassin's pistol at his head . . . . "In the present work, for the first time in a systematic and a fairly complete way, is set forth the inward history of our Revolution—the history of its ideas, its spiritual moods, its motives, its passions, even of its sportive caprices and its whims, as these uttered themselves at the time, whether consciously or not, in the various writings of the two parties of Americans who promoted or resisted that great movement. . . . The chief purpose is to call attention to these writings, not so much for their independent artistic value as for their humanistic and historical value, interpreting, as they do, with direct and undisguised speech, the very spirit and life and inward process of the American Revolution."

See preceding entry. Archie H. Jones has edited an abridged edition of Tyler's four volumes entitled *A History of American Literature, 1607-1783* (Chicago: University of Chicago Press, 1967; P).

206. Van Doren, Carl. *The American Novel, 1789-1939*. 1921. Rev. and enl. ed., New York: Macmillan, 1940.

The first full-length study of the American novel, Van Doren's work attempts to present the "record of the national imagination as exhibited in the progress of native fiction." It is largely historical in focus, and concentrates on Cooper, Hawthorne, Howells, Mark Twain, and Henry James.

207. Waggoner, Hyatt H. *American Poets: From the Puritans to the Present*. Boston: Houghton Mifflin, 1968. P (Dell).

A chronological author-by-author discussion of fifty-two "representative" American poets from Anne Bradstreet to Robert Kelly. The study is informed by the notion, which came as a surprise to its author, that "Emerson is the central figure in American poetry, essential both as spokesman and catalyst, not only the founder of the chief 'line' in our poetry but essential for an understanding of those poets not numbered among his poetic sons." (It comes as no surprise that Professor Waggoner's latest book is *Emerson as Poet* [1974].)

"From the beginning, the most representative American poets have anticipated the characteristic that more than anything else distinguishes the American poetry of our own day from that of the past and of other societies: in it *nothing* is known, nothing given, everything is discovered or created, or else remains in doubt."

208. Walcutt, Charles Child. *American Literary Naturalism: A Divided Stream*. Minneapolis: University of Minnesota Press, 1956.

"My thesis is that naturalism is the offspring of transcendentalism. American transcendentalism asserts the unity of Spirit and Nature and affirms that intuition (by which the mind discovers its affiliation with Spirit) and scientific investigation (by which it masters Nature, the symbol of Spirit) are equally rewarding and valid approaches to reality. When this mainstream of transcendentalism divides, as it does toward the end of the nineteenth century, it produces two rivers of thought. One, the approach to Spirit through intuition, nourishes idealism, progressivism, and social radicalism. The other, the approach to Nature through science, plunges into the dark canyon of mechanistic determinism. The one is rebellious, the other pessimistic; the one ardent, the other fatal; the one acknowledges will, the other denies it. Thus 'naturalism,' flowing in both streams, is partly defying Nature

84

and partly submitting to it; and it is in this area of tension that my investigation lies, its immediate subject being the forms which the novel assumes as one stream or the other, and sometimes both, flow through it. The problem, as will appear, is an epitome of the central problem of twentieth-century thought."

209.   Ward, John William. *Andrew Jackson: Symbol for an Age*. New York: Oxford University Press, 1955. P.

"The book . . . is an attempt to discover the attitudes and values of the mass of ordinary, inarticulate men in early nineteenth-century American culture through an examination of the themes and imagery that clustered about the figure of Andrew Jackson. The book is not a study of Andrew Jackson; it is a study of popular ideology. . . . The chief function of the celebration of Andrew Jackson was to project upon the man, Andrew Jackson, concepts that defined the values of the American society of his time; not to describe Andrew Jackson, so much as to affirm the validity and efficacy of the values themselves. Jackson's success was used to provide sanctions for continuing belief in the values he was understood to embody. . . . Jackson's public meaning lay in the fact that he dramatized the tension between opposites in the public mind. To take the immediate instance [of the book's tripartite organization], 'Nature' was to be understood in relation to its opposite, 'civilization.' The concept of 'Will' was divided between Promethean self-reliance and a humane regard for others; 'Providence' between the fatalism of acquiescence and the necessity for personal striving" (from Ward's auto-review in *The Historian's Workshop* [1970]).

Also of interest is President (of Amherst College) Ward's *Red, White, and Blue: Men, Books, and Ideas in American Culture* (1969).

210.   Wegelin, Christof, ed. *The American Novel: Criticism and Background Readings*. New York: Free Press, 1972. P.

Contains approximately four critical articles on each of fourteen well-known American novels, together with readings in two general areas: "The American Novel and American Experience" and "Romance, Realism, and Naturalism."

211.   Westbrook, Max, ed. *The Modern American Novel: Essays in Criticism*. New York: Random House, 1966. P.

Fourteen articles by various critics on specific works of eleven twentieth-century American authors.

212. Williams, Stanley T. *The Beginnings of American Poetry*. Uppsala, Sweden: Almqvist & Wiksells Boktryckeri Ab, 1951. Rpt. Folcroft, Pa.: Folcroft Press, 1969; New York: Cooper Square Publishers, 1970.

   A revision of lectures given at Uppsala in 1947-48, the book is concerned with the poetry of America's "cultural adolescence," the period from 1620 to 1855. It is divided into four chapters: "The Poet of Puritanism" (Bradstreet, Taylor); "The Poet of the Enlightenment" (Freneau); "The Poet of Early Romanticism" (Bryant, Longfellow, Poe); "The Poet of Philosophic Thought" (Emerson).

213. Wilson, Edmund. *Patriotic Gore: Studies in the Literature of the American Civil War*. New York: Oxford University Press, 1962. P (Galaxy Book).

   "The period of the American Civil War was not one in which belles lettres flourished, but it did produce a remarkable literature which mostly consists of speeches and pamphlets, private letters and diaries, personal memoirs and journalistic reports. . . . Such documents dramatize the war as the poet or writer of fiction has never been able to do." Cf. **75**.

   Wilson's other works include *Axel's Castle: A Study in the Imaginative Literature of 1870 to 1930* (1931), *The Triple Thinkers* (1938; rev. ed., 1948), *To the Finland Station* (1940), *The Wound and the Bow* (1941), and a four-volume chronicle of essays on American and European literature since the early twenties: *The Shores of Light: A Literary Chronicle of the Twenties and Thirties* (1952), *Classics and Commercials: A Literary Chronicle of the Forties* (1950), *The Bit between My Teeth: A Literary Chronicle of 1950-1965* (1965), and *The Devils and Canon Barham* (1973).

214. Winters, Yvor. *In Defense of Reason*. Denver: Alan Swallow, 1947. P.

   Largely a collection of the essays on American poetry and prose which had appeared in three earlier books by Winters: *Primitivism and Decadence* (1937), *Maule's Curse* (1938), and *The Anatomy of Nonsense* (1943).

   "There have been various ideas regarding the nature and function of literature during the twenty-five hundred years or so that literature has been seriously discussed . . . the didactic, the hedonistic, and the romantic. I am not in sympathy with any of these, but with a fourth, which for lack of a better term I call the moralistic. . . .

"The theory of literature which I defend in these essays is absolutist. I believe that the work of literature, in so far as it is valuable, approximates a real apprehension and communication of a particular kind of objective truth. . . . The poet makes his statement in such a way as to employ both concept and connotation as efficiently as possible. The poem is good in so far as it makes a defensible rational statement about a given human experience (the experience need not be real but must be in some sense possible) and at the same time communicates the emotion which ought to be motivated by that rational understanding of that experience. . . . [In addition] a poem, in so far as it is good, represents the comprehension on a moral plane of a given experience."

215. Wright, Louis B. *The Cultural Life of the American Colonies, 1607-1763.* New American Nation Series. New York: Harper, 1957.

"His book [according to Commager and Morris, editors of the series] is concerned not with traditional political history but with depicting how the colonists lived, the faiths and goals that inspired them, and the manner in which their lives were enriched. . . . The cultural life of the colonies produced no Shakespeare, no Rembrandt, no Newton, and no Handel. Benjamin Franklin stands alone as the cultural giant of colonial times. But much of this age was devoted not to thought but to action, to clearing the wilderness and establishing military security. Once these basic goals were achieved the level of cultural attainment rose extraordinarily fast, as evidenced by the expansion and quality of the literary output, the notable level of the achievement in the household and decorative arts, the widening horizon of scientific interests, and the advance of higher education."

See also Wright's *The Arts in America: The Colonial Period* (1966).

216. Young, Thomas D., and Ronald E. Fine. *American Literature: A Critical Survey.* 2 vols. New York: American Book Co., 1968. P.

Forty-eight relatively recent essays on nineteen major American writers.

217. Zabel, Morton Dauwen, ed. *Literary Opinion in America: Essays Illustrating the Status, Methods, and Problems of Criticism in the United States in the Twentieth Century.* 2 vols. 1937. 3rd ed., New York: Harper, 1962.

Seventy-eight essays by fifty-five critics covering the years from 1890 to 1950.

218. Ziff, Larzer. *The American 1890's: Life and Times of a Lost Generation.* New York: Viking, 1966. P (Compass Book).

"By the beginning of the nineties Whitman's dream was bankrupt, and Melville saved himself the pain of speaking out. What had intervened to guarantee them loneliness in their old age was a wholesale commercialization of life. It did not deny literature. Rather, it granted literature a place and in so doing reduced it far more than organized denial could have done." The young writers of the nineties (Garland, Bierce, Stephen Crane, Norris, Dreiser) opposed such commercialism as well as the gentility represented by Lowell, Holmes, and Whittier. Although these young writers lost the battle for literary influence in their day, "modern American literary men were to look to the defeated of the nineties as their true precursors."

III Reference Works

225. Berrey, Lester V., and Melvin Van den Bark. *The American Thesaurus of Slang: A Complete Reference Book of Colloquial Speech*. 1942. 2nd ed., New York: Crowell, 1953.

   Elaborate categories and thesaurus organization (Berrey is the editor of the latest revision of *Roget's Thesaurus*) make the work difficult to use, in spite of a 370-page index. See **10, 151, 230, 238,** and especially **243.**

226. *Books in Print: An Author-Title Series Index to the Publishers' Trade List Annual*. 2 vols.: *Authors* and *Titles and Publishers*. New York: Bowker.
   Paperbound Books in Print. New York: Bowker.

   Indispensable (but occasionally inaccurate) lists of books available in America. *Books in Print*, published annually, includes paperbacks. *Paperbound Books in Print* is published twice a year in hardbound volumes divided into title, author, and subject entries. The most recent volume, December 1974, lists 123,000 titles. Cf. **234.**

227. Carruth, Gorton, et al. *The Encyclopedia of American Facts and Dates*. 5th ed. New York: Crowell, 1970.

   "The three chief purposes of *The Encyclopedia of American Facts and Dates* are to present in one volume a vast number of the most interesting events from America's past, to arrange these events both in chronological and at the same time concurrent order, and finally to provide a complete cross-referenced index for instant and easy consulting."

228. *Contemporary Authors: The International Bio-Bibliographical Guide to Current Authors and Their Works*. Detroit, Mich.: Gale Research Co., 1962—.

   Contains biographical and brief bibliographical information on about 22,000 American authors born since 1900, including over 3,000 writers still in their twenties and thirties. The publisher claims that "75% of the authors in *CA* are not listed in other major reference works." Published quarterly to

1964, semiannually thereafter, each volume now contains about 3,500 new entries arranged alphabetically. A fully cumulative index, indispensable in using this on-going series, is published each year. Earlier volumes are revised and updated at five- to ten-year intervals. See next entry.

229.   *Contemporary Poets* (1971), *Contemporary Novelists* (1972), and *Contemporary Dramatists* (1973). Contemporary Writers Series. Ed. James Vinson. London: St. James Press; New York: St. Martin's Press.

The series "provides biographical, bibliographical and critical information on some 1,100 poets, 600 novelists and 300 dramatists from Great Britain and Ireland, the United States and Canada, Australia and New Zealand, and Africa, Asia and the West Indies. . . . Each volume will be revised every three years." See previous entry.

230.   Craigie, William A., and James R. Hulbert. *A Dictionary of American English on Historical Principles*. 4 vols. Chicago: University of Chicago Press, 1938-44.

To exhibit "clearly those features by which the English of the American colonies and the United States is distinguished from that of England and the rest of the English-speaking world . . . as fully as possible is one of the chief aims of the present . . . work, which includes, however, not only words and phrases which are clearly or apparently of American origin, or have greater currency here than elsewhere, but also every word denoting something which has a real connection with the development of the country and the history of its people. . . . The end of the nineteenth century has been selected as a fitting point at which to terminate the admission of new words, however common some of these may have become in recent use. The illustration of those already current before that date, however, is frequently carried into the first quarter of the present century. It has also been found necessary to restrict the inclusion of slang and dialect words to those which are of early date or special prominence." See **10, 151, 225, 238, 243.**

231.   *Dictionary of American Biography*. 20 vols., with a separate *Index*. New York: Scribner's, 1928-37. Rpt. in 13 vols., n.d. *Supplement One* (1944), *Supplement Two* (1958), *Supplement Three* (1973).

First underwritten by Adolph Ochs of the New York *Times*,

the *DAB* is modeled on the British *Dictionary of National Biography*. It is the standard guide to the lives of deceased Americans who have made "some significant contribution" to the national life. In 1928 the *DAB* took some pride in including biographies of industrialists, scientists, and artists, whereas "earlier collections [had] stressed . . . principally lives of soldiers, statesmen, and clergymen." Its entries attempt "not only to state but to appraise the circumstances and influences which shaped careers" and to provide not just "a bare narrative of events, but . . . a definite impression of personality and achievements."

Supplement One (with coverage of Americans who died between 1928 and 1935), *Supplement Two* (coverage from 1935 to 1940), and *Supplement Three* (coverage from 1941 to 1945) were undertaken "to maintain the *Dictionary* as a living and continuing enterprise." They are individually indexed (with a composite index to all three supplements in *Supplement Three*) and retain the form and intent of the original *Dictionary*. There is also a one-volume abridgment, *Concise Dictionary of American Biography* (1964).

Other biographical dictionaries, useful for obscure authors, include *The National Cyclopedia of American Biography* (67 vols., 1891—); Oscar F. Adams, *A Dictionary of American Authors* (1884; 5th ed. rev. and enl., 1905); *Appletons' Cyclopaedia of American Biography* (7 vols., 1887-1900); W. J. Burke and Will D. Howe, *American Authors and Books: 1640 to the Present Day* (1943; 3rd ed., rev. Irving and Anne Weiss, 1972); W. Stewart Wallace, *Dictionary of North American Authors Deceased before 1950* (1951); and the several volumes produced by Stanley J. Kunitz and Howard Haycraft: *American Authors* (1938; coverage from 1600 to 1900); *Twentieth Century Authors* (1942; rpt. 1966); *Twentieth Century Authors: First Supplement* (1955). A one-volume *Encyclopedia of American Biography*, ed. J.A. Garraty and J.L. Sternstein, was published by Harper & Row in 1974. Cf. **17, 25, 48, 228, 229, 242.**

232.   Follett, Wilson. *Modern American Usage: A Guide*. Edited and completed by Jacques Barzun et al. New York: Hill & Wang, 1966. P (Paperback Library).

A reasonably successful attempt to produce an American species of the genus Fowler. See **241**.

233.   *Guide to Microforms in Print*. Englewood, Colo.: Microcard Editions, 1961—.

A softbound annual which "lists over 25,000 books, journals, newspapers, and multi-volume sets available on microfilm (16mm. and 35mm.), microfiche and micro-opaque cards from publishers in the United States." Entries give author, title, publisher, price, and type of microform used. NCR also publishes a separate annual *Subject Guide to Microforms in Print*.

234. *Guide to Reprints*. Englewood, Colo.: Microcard Editions, 1967—.

A softbound annual which currently lists over 77,000 volumes reprinted by 542 domestic and foreign publishers. Each entry includes author, title, date of original publication, reprint publisher, and current price.

235. Hart, James D. *The Oxford Companion to American Literature*. 4th ed. New York: Oxford University Press, 1965.

A thousand-page alphabetical encyclopedia "to the authors and writings, past and present, popular and polite, that are included in the area of American literature . . .[and to] major nonliterary aspects of the American mind and the American scene as these are reflected in and influenced by American literature." See **236**.

236. Herzberg, Max J. *The Reader's Encyclopedia of American Literature*. New York: Crowell, 1962.

"This volume [stated Van Wyck Brooks, in an introduction written shortly before his death] touches on virtually every subject that is related to American literature. It includes biographical sketches of authors, bibliographies, and articles, short or long, on the social background of American writing, its schools and movements . . . on magazines, editors and statesmen, famous characters in fiction, folk heroes, historical events. With entries, as well, on novels and poems, and essays on various types of writing, this comprehensive handbook covers its wide-ranging subject with remarkable thoroughness."

Herzberg's 1,300-page volume is broader in scope and occasionally more penetrating in interpretation than Hart's similar *Oxford Companion to American Literature* (**235**).

237. Holman, C. Hugh. *A Handbook to Literature*. 3rd ed. Indianapolis: Bobbs-Merrill, 1972.

Alphabetical handbooks of literary terms are not currently in fashion, and possibly for good reason. The student interested in "irony" or "humor" or "realism" is not likely to be satisfied with a one- or two-page definition. Nevertheless, there is perhaps still a place for a reference work—and Holman's book, based on the 1936 original by William Flint Thrall and Addison Hubbard, is one of the best—which can refresh one's grasp of the distinctions between zeugma and syllepsis, metonymy and synecdoche, and provide introductory discussions of the antinovel, the Connecticut wits, and New Criticism. The most recent edition includes literary terms, genres, movements, and periods, as well as an outline of English and American literary history and lists of winners of National Book Awards, Nobel Prizes for Literature, and Pulitzer Prizes.

Also of interest are the *Dictionary of World Literature* (Patterson, N.J.: Littlefield, Adams, 1960), ed. Joseph T. Shipley with substantial short essays by several hundred scholars; and M. H. Abrams' brief but perceptive *Glossary of Literary Terms* (New York: Holt, Rinehart and Winston, 1957).

238. Mathews, Mitford M. *A Dictionary of Americanisms on Historical Principles.* Chicago: University of Chicago Press, 1951.

An attempt to catalogue all words with a "history in print" coined by Americans, containing some 50,000 entries. In 1966 Mathews published an abridgment entitled *Americanisms: A Dictionary of Selected Americanisms on Historical Principles,* which lists 1,000 entries of special interest (available in both cloth and paper from the University of Chicago Press). See **10, 151, 225, 230, 243.**

239. *MLA Style Sheet.* 2nd ed. Rev. William R. Parker, John H. Fisher, et al. New York: The Modern Language Association of America, 1970. P.

"Since its publication in April 1951, the *MLA Style Sheet* has been very widely adopted by journals, presses, and graduate and undergraduate departments as a standard for the style of documentation in the humanities. . . . Since the rules in the *MLA Style Sheet* have been so widely accepted, substantive change in the revised edition has been kept to a minimum." Copies may be obtained from the Materials Center, Modern Language Association, 62 Fifth Ave., New York, N.Y. 10011.

For a more comprehensive discussion of style, especially that of a book manuscript, the student and the prospective author may wish to consult *A Manual of Style* (12th ed., rev., Chicago: University of Chicago Press, 1969).

240.   Morris, Richard B. *Encyclopedia of American History*. Enl. and
           updated ed. New York: Harper & Row, 1970.
           "The aim of this encyclopedia is to provide in a single handy
           volume the essential historical facts about American life and
           institutions. The organization is both chronological and topi-
           cal."

241.   Nicholson, Margaret. *A Dictionary of American-English Usage*.
           New York: Oxford University Press, 1957. P.
           An "adaptation" of H. W. Fowler's classic *Dictionary of Mod-
           ern English Usage* (1926). "AEU is a simplified MEU, with
           American variations, retaining as much of the original as
           space allowed." See **232**.

242.   *Notable American Women, 1607-1950: A Biographical Dictionary*.
           Ed. Edward T. James. 3 vols. Cambridge, Mass.: Harvard
           University Press, 1971.
           Contains 1,359 entries on women "whose lives and careers
           have had significant impact on American life in all fields of
           thought and action." Modeled on and in spirit a supplement
           to the *Dictionary of American Biography* (**231**), since "that work,
           distinguished as it is, included no more than 700 biographies
           of women out of a total of nearly 15,000 entries."

243.   Wentworth, Harold, and Stuart Berg Flexner. *Dictionary of
           American Slang*. New York: Crowell, 1960.
           "American slang, as used in the title of this dictionary, is the
           body of words and expressions frequently used by or intellig-
           ible to a rather large portion of the general American public,
           but not accepted as good, formal usage by the majority. . . .
           [It] tries for a quick, easy, personal mode of speech. It comes
           mostly from cant, jargon, and argot words and expressions
           whose popularity has increased until a large number of the
           general public uses or understands them. Much of this slang
           retains a basic characteristic of its origin: it is *fully* intelligible
           only to initiates."
           The standard work on American slang, this volume has the
           advantage over Berrey and Van den Bark (**225**) of the dictio-
           nary over the thesaurus. Students of American and English
           slang should also be familiar with Eric Partridge's *A Dictionary
           of Slang and Unconventional English* (rev., enl. 7th ed., 2 vols. in
           1, New York: Macmillan, 1970). Cf. **10, 151, 230, 238**.

IV Editions and Series

256. The Anchor Documents in American Civilization Series. Hennig Cohen and John William Ward, general eds. New York: Doubleday. P.

"The purpose of this series is to provide primary material for the study of the history of the United States and for the understanding of American culture. In content, each book [contains] such written documents as diaries, newspaper editorials, autobiographies and histories, textbooks and popular fiction, along with pictorial documents." The series includes *American Life in the 1840's* (ed. Carl Bode); *The American Literary Revolution, 1783-1837* (ed. Robert E. Spiller); *Ideology and Power in the Age of Jackson* (ed. Edwin C. Rozwenc); *The 1940's: Profile of a Nation in Crisis* (ed. Chester E. Eisinger); *Popular Culture and Industrialism, 1865-1890* (ed. Henry Nash Smith); and *The Strenuous Decade: A Social and Intellectual Record of the 1930's* (ed. Daniel Aaron and Robert Bendiner).

257. Braziller. The American Culture series. New York. P.

A series of documents and illustrations which attempts to "reconstruct the color and variety of our cultural heritage." Includes *Remarkable Providences, 1600-1760; The Rising Glory, 1760-1820; Notions of the Americans, 1820-1860; Democratic Vistas, 1860-1880; The Land of Contrasts, 1880-1901; The Call of the Wild, 1900-1916; The Plastic Age, 1917-1930; Culture and Commitment, 1929-1945*.

258. Chandler Facsimile Series in American Literature. San Francisco: Chandler Publishing Co. P.

Facsimile reprints of first editions of major works. "Each work is preceded by a critical introduction, biographical and textual notes, and a bibliography." Presently available are *Maggie: A Girl of the Streets* (1893 ed.), *Leaves of Grass, The Confidence-Man, The Scarlet Letter, Pudd'nhead Wilson and Those Extraordinary Twins* (American Publishing Co. ed., 1894), *Adventures of Huckleberry Finn, A Connecticut Yankee in King Arthur's Court, Nature*.

259.   The Chicago History of American Civilization. Ed. Daniel
Boorstin. Chicago: University of Chicago Press.

Contains two kinds of books: a chronological group, which
will provide a coherent narrative of American history from its
beginning to the present day [e.g., Edmund S. Morgan, *The
Birth of the Republic: 1763-89*; John Hope Franklin, *Reconstruction: After the Civil War*], and a topical group which will deal
with the history of varied and significant aspects of American
life [such as Richard M. Dorson, *American Folklore*; Bernard A.
Weisberger, *The American Newspaperman*; Irving Sablosky,
American Music; and William T. Hagan, *American Indians*]."

260.   Columbia University Press. Introductions to Twentieth-
Century American Poetry. New York.

A new series of interpretative volumes devoted to individual authors. "The primary interest in the books is on the
way the poetry of the writer under study has evolved, the
principal themes it touches on, and the way it relates to larger
movements in contemporary literature or thought." Included thus far are Ezra Pound, Marianne Moore, Theodore
Roethke, and Hart Crane.

261.   Gale Research Co. Modern Authors Checklist Series. Detroit.

Provides bibliographical descriptions of works by (but not
about) twentieth-century authors. Thus far, the series includes volumes on James Dickey, James Gould Cozzens, Kenneth Millar/Ross MacDonald, Kurt Vonnegut, Jr., Nelson
Algren, and Robert Lowell.

Gale also publishes an Authors at Auction Series and has
announced a four-volume guide to first editions of American
authors entitled *First Printings of American Authors*. The Gale
Information Guide Library projects a massive series of bibliographies in the social sciences, humanities, and current
affairs, including volumes on American fiction, Afro-
American fiction, American drama, American poetry, the
literary journal in America, little magazines, and American
prose and criticism. The first book in this series, James Woodress' *American Fiction, 1900-1950*, was released early in 1975
(dated 1974). It contains an intermittently annotated list of
source material followed by very brief descriptions of the
works, editions, biographies, and criticisms of forty-four
twentieth-century American authors.

262. Goldentree Bibliographies. New York: Appleton-Century-Crofts.

For bibliographies of American literature, the American novel, American drama, and Afro-American writers, see **13, 18, 32, 40, 47,** and **62**. There are also Goldentree Bibliographies in American history (the American colonies, the American Revolution, the Civil War, the Gilded Age, history of American education, American economic history, American social history, religion in American life, the Progressive era, and others).

263. Hall (as agent for Twayne). Two series: American Author Bibliographies and Reference Guides in American Literature. Boston: announced for 1974.

"Bibliographical reference guides on all important American authors [which] provide entries for critical and secondary studies about authors and their works and, when appropriate, include information about primary works and major library collections."

264. Heath. Problems in American Civilization. Ed. Edwin C. Rozwenc. Lexington, Mass. P.

A series of pamphlets which reprint central—and usually conflicting—documents concerning significant issues in American life (e.g., *Puritanism in Early America, The Role of the Frontier, Individualism and Conformity in the American Character*).

265. Charles E. Merrill Checklists. Columbus, Ohio. P.

Brief (approximately forty-page), unannotated lists of individual authors' works and secondary scholarship and criticism. Each checklist is divided into six sections: "Books and Separate Publications," "Editions," "Letters," "Bibliographies," "Biographies," "Scholarship and Criticism." Twenty-two checklists have been published so far, covering, for the most part, standard American authors. In addition to the checklists, Merrill also publishes Standard Editions, Studies, Guides, and Literary Texts, as part of a smorgasbord Merrill Program in American Literature.

266. Modern Language Association. Center for Editions of American Authors (CEAA).

The "greatest cooperative project in American literary scholarship . . . the CEAA is presently directing work on . . . definitive editions of nineteenth-century American authors": Charles Brockden Brown (Kent State University Press),

Stephen Crane (University Press of Virginia), John Dewey (Southern Illinois University Press), Ralph Waldo Emerson (two series: Journals and Miscellaneous Notebooks, in twelve volumes; and Works; both by Harvard University Press), Washington Irving (University of Wisconsin Press), William Dean Howells (Indiana University Press), William James (Harvard University Press), James Russell Lowell (Northern Illinois University Press), Herman Melville (Northwestern University Press), William Gilmore Simms (University of South Carolina Press), Henry David Thoreau (Princeton University Press), Mark Twain (two series: Papers, previously unpublished, University of California Press; Works, previously published, Iowa/California university presses); Walt Whitman (New York University Press). These thirteen university presses and some two hundred scholars, supported by NEH and USOE grants, have thus far produced 118 volumes (out of a projected total of 260) which "attempt to establish 'definitive' texts of an author's works—texts prepared through the collation of the various published and unpublished forms of these works produced during the author's lifetime that reflect his final intentions with regard to his works."

A volume of essays celebrating the project and reappraising some of the authors—*The Chief Glory of Every People*, edited by CEAA director Matthew J. Bruccoli—was published by Southern Illinois University Press in 1973. For a contrary opinion, see Edmund Wilson's "Fruits of the MLA," published in the *New York Review of Books* (26 Sept., 10 Oct. 1968) and collected in *The Devils and Canon Barham* (see **213**).

When NEH grant support terminates in August 1976, the work of the CEAA will be carried forward by a new Center for Scholarly Editions. . According to the MLA Executive Council, "this new CSE, directed by a seven-member standing committee and coordinated by a staff associate at MLA Headquarters, will continue the work of the CEAA in maintaining high standards and awarding a CSE emblem for scholarly editions, but unlike the CEAA, it will not be a funding agency and will not limit its efforts to editions involving American authors."

267. Norton Critical Editions. New York. P.

Each edition reprints an authoritative text together with source materials and a selection of critical essays. The series now includes *Adventures of Huckleberry Finn, The Confidence-*

Man, The Red Badge of Courage, Sister Carrie, The House of the Seven Gables, The Scarlet Letter, The Ambassadors, The Turn of the Screw, Moby-Dick, Walden and Civil Disobedience, Leaves of Grass, and *The Portrait of a Lady.*

268. Pegasus American Authors. New York: Western Publishing Co.

A new series of critical biographies of major twentieth-century American writers. Volumes produced thus far include studies of Robinson and G. W. Cable.

269. Pittsburgh Series in Bibliography. Pittsburgh: University of Pittsburgh Press.

Thus far the series includes descriptive bibliographies of Hart Crane, F. Scott Fitzgerald, Wallace Stevens, Eugene O'Neill, and John Berryman.

270. Popular American Literature. Indianapolis: Odyssey Press. P.

This series now includes five volumes: *Seth Jones* (Edward S. Ellis) and *Deadwood Dick on Deck* (Edward L. Wheeler); *Ten Nights in a Bar-Room* (T. S. Arthur) and *In His Steps* (Charles M. Sheldon); *Adrift in New York* and *The World before Him* (both by Horatio Alger); *Tempest and Sunshine* (Mary Jane Holmes) and *The Lamplighter* (Maria Susanna Cummins); *The Monks of Monk Hall* (George Lippard).

271. Prentice-Hall. Film Focus series. Ed. Ronald Gottesman and Harry M. Geduld. Englewood Cliffs, N.J. P.

Contains collections of articles on individual films, genres, and directors. Volumes published thus far include *Birth of a Nation, Bonnie and Clyde, Chaplin, D. W. Griffith, Citizen Kane, Howard Hawks, Hitchcock,* and *The Western*.

272. Prentice-Hall. Twentieth Century Views. Englewood Cliffs, N.J. P.

A series of collections of short critical pieces on individual authors which presents "contemporary critical opinion" on such major writers as Edward Albee, James Baldwin, Saul Bellow, Stephen Crane, e. e. cummings, Emily Dickinson, T. S. Eliot, Ralph Ellison, Emerson, Faulkner, Fitzgerald, Frost, Hawthorne, Hemingway, Henry James, Sinclair Lewis, Robert Lowell, Malamud, Mailer, Melville, Arthur Miller, Modern Black Poets, Marianne Moore, O'Neill, Poe, Pound, Robinson, Steinbeck, Stevens, Thoreau, Thurbur, Mark Twain, Edith Wharton, Nathaniel West, Whitman, W. C.

Williams, and Thomas Wolfe. Several volumes are devoted to genres, e.g., *The Modern American Theater*.

A companion paperbound series, Twentieth Century Interpretations, is composed of collections of critical essays devoted to individual works. Included thus far are volumes on *Absalom, Absalom!*, *The Adventures of Huckleberry Finn*, *The Ambassadors*, *Arrowsmith*, *Billy Budd*, *The Crucible*, *The Fall of the House of Usher*, *A Farewell to Arms*, *The Great Gatsby*, *The Iceman Cometh*, *Invisible Man*, *Light in August*, *Miss Lonelyhearts*, *Murder in the Cathedral*, *Native Son*, *The Old Man and the Sea*, Poe's *Tales*, *The Portrait of a Lady*, *The Scarlet Letter*, *The Sound and the Fury*, *A Streetcar Named Desire*, *The Turn of the Screw and Other Tales*, *Walden*, and *The Waste Land*.

273. Routledge & Kegan Paul. Critical Heritage Series. London.

Each volume is a collection of chronologically arranged reviews, letters, and diary entries dealing with the major works of the author under consideration (Cooper, Stephen Crane, Melville, Pound, and Mark Twain thus far), and especially useful for the compilation of critical opinion published during the author's lifetime.

274. The Serif Series of Bibliographies and Checklists. Kent, Ohio: Kent State University Press.

A series originally spawned by *The Serif*, a bibliographical quarterly published at Kent State. The series includes bibliographies and checklists of varying length (35 to 293 pages) on various authors (Edward Taylor to Dashiell Hammett) and topics (published screenplays; science fiction criticism). To date, twenty-nine volumes have been published.

275. The Twayne United States Authors Series. New York. P (College and University Press).

A continuing series (240 volumes thus far) of introductory critical biographies of medium length (about 150 pages) and widely varying quality. Each volume contains a "Selected Bibliography."

276. University of Miami Press. Readings in Literary Criticism. Coral Gables, Fla.

Collections of diverse critical opinions (entitled *Critics on*——) on standard American authors (thus far—Emerson, Mark Twain, Poe, Melville, Whitman, Emily Dickinson, Ezra Pound, Hawthorne, Robert Lowell, Henry James, Wallace Stevens). Each volume includes a bibliography.

277. University of Minnesota Pamphlets on American Writers. Minneapolis. P.

A biographical-critical series which now includes 103 titles on individual American writers and topics (such as *The American Short Story, Recent American Poetry, American Humorists*). About forty-eight pages each, including bibliography.

278. Viking Portable Library. New York. P.

Collections of fiction, supplemented by essays, letters, and autobiography, available for seventeen major and minor American authors (and one composite collection, the *North American Indian Reader,* **319**). Of special interest in this series is Malcolm Cowley's edition of Faulkner's writings, originally published in 1946, which first called attention to the importance of the totality of Faulkner's works, of the mythic and epic significance of the many writings that together constitute the chronicle of Yoknapatawpha. ("The job is splendid," wrote Faulkner to Cowley. "Damn you to hell anyway. . . . I didn't know myself what I had tried to do, and how much I had succeeded.") Other volumes concern Sherwood Anderson, Saul Bellow, Clemens, Stephen Crane, Emerson, Hawthorne, James, Melville, Arthur Miller, Nabokov, Dorothy Parker, Poe, Prescott, Steinbeck, Thoreau, Veblen, and Whitman.

There are also Viking Critical Library editions (which include biographical, bibliographical, and other related material) available for *Winesburg, Ohio; Death of a Salesman; The Crucible; The Grapes of Wrath*; and *One Flew over the Cuckoo's Nest.*

279. Western Writers Series. Boise, Idaho: Boise State University. P.

"This continuing series, primarily regional in nature, provides brief [fifty-page] introductions to the lives and works of authors who have written significant literature about the American West." A less successful regional version of the Minnesota Pamphlets (**277**).

V Anthologies

Recent anthologies which cover the full span of American literature include those published by Norton (1956; 4th ed., 1974); Viking (1962; 3rd ed., 1975); Holt, Rinehart and Winston (1965); Odyssey Press (1965); Washington Square Press (1966); Heath (1969); Houghton Mifflin (1970); McGraw-Hill (1970); Free Press (1971); St. Martin's Press (1973); and Macmillan (1974).

The three best are the Norton (*The American Tradition in Literature*, ed. Bradley, Beatty, and Long), Macmillan (*Anthology of American Literature*, ed. McMichael), and St. Martin's (*American Literature: The Makers and the Making*, ed. Cleanth Brooks, Robert Penn Warren, and R. W. B. Lewis). The St. Martin's Press edition contains remarkably perceptive critical introductions for a comprehensive anthology. In addition to a conventional two-volume set, split by the Civil War, it is available in four paperback volumes, which make it possible to use the second and third volumes for a nineteenth-century course and to assign individual volumes as supplementary texts in shorter period courses.

285.   Allen, Gay Wilson, Walter B. Rideout, and James K. Robinson, eds. *American Poetry.* New York: Harper & Row, 1965.

An anthology which includes an extensive section listing— for individual poets—bibliographies, standard editions, biographies, and major critical books and articles.

286.   Baker, Houston A., Jr. *Black Literature in America.* New York: McGraw-Hill, 1971. P.

"Existing standards are fine as far as they go, but they cannot serve as the sole criteria for determining the worthy or unworthy in a body of literature that was largely ignored when the standards were being formulated. . . . The vast and accomplished body of black American folklore remains in view throughout the [anthology] because it seems to me that black American literature, like all other bodies of literature, develops from a folkloristic base and constantly manifests its dependence on the folk base in its conscious works of litera-

ture. I have also stressed sociohistorical concerns throughout."

287. Blair, Walter. *Native American Humor*. San Francisco: Chandler Publishing Co., 1960. P. Originally published in 1937 as
Native American Humor (1800-1900).

This influential work helped to establish the
significance—and the legitimacy—of the nineteenth-century
humorists. The 1960 edition adds a new chapter, "Aftermath:
Twentieth-Century Humorists," to the book-length (180-
page) introduction and updates the original bibliography.
Both introduction and anthology are organized in sections
on "Down East Humor (1830-1867)," "Humor of the Old
Southwest (1830-1867)," "Literary Comedians (1855-1900),"
"The Local Colorists (1868-1900)," and "Mark Twain." Cf.
291 and **301**.

Walter Blair is also the author of *Horse Sense in American
Humor* (1942); *Half Horse, Half Alligator: The Growth of the Mike
Fink Legend*, with F. J. Meine (1956): and *Mark Twain & Huck
Finn* (1960).

288. Bontemps, Arna. *American Negro Poetry*. 1963. Rev. ed., New
York: Hill & Wang, 1974. P (American Century Book).

The revised edition adds twelve new poets to this standard
anthology, notable for breadth of coverage (now sixty-eight
poets) rather than depth (most poets are represented by a
half-dozen poems, or fewer).

289. Cady, Edwin H. *The American Poets, 1800-1900*. Glenview, Ill.:
Scott, Foresman, 1966. P.

"The emergence of Modern seems to have required something like a classically Freudian act of patricide. The indispensable confidence of the newness stood upon the
slaughtered reputations of bearded Fireside and Schoolroom
poets and 'Victorians' at large. A generation later, however,
we have no need to continue in the superstitions of the past.
The modernist fight is over and its victory consummated; we
may look with different eyes to the condition of its ancient
adversary. . . . There are 'old standard' poets (Bryant, Whittier, Holmes, Lowell) and 'new standard' poets who are to us
much more interesting than they appeared to their contem-
poraneous publics (Boker, Tuckerman, Thoreau, Melville,
Crane). The balancing of such an equation demands recognition of a 'perennially standard' group—poets who despite

critical raid and foray and the passage of fads and schools
have stayed in favorable view: Poe, Emerson, Longfellow
(renewedly), Whitman, Dickinson, Robinson."

290. Coffin, Tristram Potter, and Hennig Cohen. *Folklore: From the
Working Folk of America*. Garden City, N. Y.: Doubleday, 1973.
P (Anchor Book).
"The present volume concentrates on the folklore in
American occupations—on the traditional artistic expression
of those who find their identity (at least to a large degree) in
the way they earn their living, rather than in where they live
or their racial background. Our selections, therefore, might
be called expressions of 'the arts of the crafts.' "

291. Cohen, Hennig, and William B. Dillingham. *Humor of the Old
Southwest*. 1964. 2nd ed., Athens: University of Georgia Press,
1975. P.
Selections from twenty-four authors (including Augustus
B. Longstreet, William Tappan Thompson, George
Washington Harris, Johnson Jones Hooper, T. B. Thorpe,
and their transforming heir, Mark Twain) who produced, in
the four decades from the death of Mike Fink to the Civil
War, exuberant sketches and tales of the recently settled
Southern frontier between the Savannah River and the Mississippi.
"The writers were not themselves the rugged, illiterate but
imaginative hearties who told their yarns but never wrote
them down. They were educated men who seldom broke the
wilderness, although they were close to it. From the roarers,
from literary sources such as eighteenth-century essayists,
from the tales of Baron Munchausen, and even from such
contemporaries as Washington Irving, these men formed a
new kind of literature, chiefly anecdotal in nature but with a
freshness in language and a boldness in detail which stands as
a foundation for modern American writing." Cf. **287** and
301.

292. Conron, John J. *The American Landscape*. New York: Oxford
University Press, 1974. P.
"Over 130 selections of prose and poetry chronicle the
changing American landscape. They form both a historical
and literary record of the physical and perceptual transformation of the land from a New World seen as a Paradise to a
world deformed and defaced by modern technology."

293.   Duffey, Bernard I. *Modern American Literature.* New York: Holt, Rinehart and Winston, 1951. P.

An anthology of twentieth-century short fiction, poetry, and essays by major American authors.

294.   Elliott, George P. *Fifteen Modern American Poets.* New York: Holt, Rinehart and Winston, 1956. P.

"This book aims to represent the middle generation of American poets": Elizabeth Bishop, Richard Eberhart, Randall Jarrell, Robert Lowell, Josephine Miles, Howard Nemerov, Hyam Plutzik, Theodore Roethke, Muriel Rukeyser, James Schevill, Delmore Schwartz, Winfield Townley Scott, Karl Shapiro, Robert Penn Warren, Richard Wilbur. .

295.   Ellmann, Richard, and Charles Feidelson, Jr. *The Modern Tradition: Backgrounds of Modern Literature.* New York: Oxford University Press, 1965. P.

"If we can postulate a modern tradition, we must add that it is a paradoxically untraditional tradition. Modernism strongly implies some sort of historical discontinuity, either a liberation from inherited patterns or, at another extreme, deprivation and disinheritance. In an essay on 'The Modern Element in Modern Literature,' Lionel Trilling singles out a radically anti-cultural bias as the most important attribute of the modern imagination. Committed to everything in human experience that militates against custom, abstract order, and even reason itself, modern literature has elevated individual existence over social man, unconscious feeling over self-conscious perception, passion and will over intellection and systematic morals, dynamic vision over the static image, dense actuality over practical reality. In these and other ways, it has made the most of its break with the past, its inborn challenge to established culture. Concurrently, it has been what Henry James called an 'imagination of disaster.' Interwoven with the access of knowledge, the experimental verve, and the personal urgency of the modern masters is, as Trilling also finds, a sense of loss, alienation, and despair. These are the two faces, positive and negative, of the modern as the anti-traditional: freedom and deprivation, a living present and a dead past. . . .

"Specifically, the materials [of this excellent 950-page anthology] consist of discursive statements by writers, artists, philosophers, and scientists" organized in nine sections on symbolism, realism, nature, cultural history, the unconscious, myth, self-consciousness, existence, and faith.

296.   Ellmann, Richard, and Robert O'Clair. *The Norton Anthology of Modern Poetry*. New York: Norton, 1973. P.

A 1,400-page collection of the poems of 158 British and American poets of the twentieth century (as well as Whitman, Dickinson, Hopkins, and Hardy). "We have included many poems by each major figure, but we have also provided a generous selection of poets less celebrated but still of commanding interest." Includes introductions, footnotes, and bibliographies.

297.   Falk, Robert P. *American Literature in Parody: A Collection of Parody, Satire, and Literary Burlesque of American Writers Past and Present*. New York: Twayne, 1955.

298.   Hills, Penney Chapin, and L. Rust Hills. *How We Live: Contemporary Life in Contemporary Fiction*. New York: Macmillan, 1968. P (2 vols., Collier).

A thousand-page collection of fifty-six short stories and portions of novels by forty-eight American writers of the last fifteen years which is, claims Malcolm Cowley, "the best existing collection of strictly contemporary fiction."

299.   Hoffman, Daniel G. *American Poetry and Poetics: Poems and Critical Documents from the Puritans to Robert Frost*. Garden City, N.Y.: Doubleday, 1962. P.

About equally divided between selections from the poetry of sixteen major American poets and essays on critical theory by poets and others.

300.   Litz, A. Walton. *Major American Short Stories*. New York: Oxford University Press, 1975.

Arranged chronologically in four sections: "The Search for Form" (Irving, Hawthorne, Poe, Melville, James); "Regionalism and Realism" (Mark Twain, Howells, Jewett, Garland); "A National Art Form" (Crane, Wharton, Anderson, Fitzgerald, Hemingway, Faulkner, Welty, Warren, Wright, Bellow, O'Connor, Malamud, Taylor, Updike); "The Short Story Today" (Oates, Barth, Barthelme, Coover, Cheever).

301.   Lynn, Kenneth S. *The Comic Tradition in America: An Anthology*. New York: Norton, 1958. P.

"With the notable exception of Benjamin Franklin, the selections are all drawn from what seems to me the great age of American humor, the nineteenth century." Professor Lynn also explores the topic of the humor of the Old Southwest, especially its political implications, in *Mark Twain and Southwestern Humor* (1959). Cf. **287** and **291**.

302. Meserole, Harrison T. *Seventeenth-Century American Poetry.* Garden City, N.Y.: Doubleday, 1968. P (Norton Library).

"Students of early America have been largely unaware of the considerable body of verse written by the men and women of our first century ... [who] used poetry as it has always been used—to tell stories, to celebrate, to mourn, to praise, commemorate, describe, instruct, and to express both sacred and profane love....

"The first [part of the anthology] contains a substantial and representative selection from the works of Edward Taylor, Anne Bradstreet, and Michael Wigglesworth.... In the second part are selections from the writings of fourteen poets who, though assiduous and competent in their art, in some significant aspect fall short of the level reached by Taylor, Bradstreet, and Wigglesworth.... The third part contains a group of writers and verse selected to represent the more than 200 other writers and their more than 1,500 poems of which we have record in America before 1725. The fourth part contains anonymous verse ... and the *Bay Psalm Book* has been represented in a separate section.... Roughly half the verse included has not been printed since the seventeenth century; 59 poems are printed here for the first time."

303. Miller, Perry, and Thomas H. Johnson. *The Puritans.* 1938. Rev. ed., 2 vols., New York: Harper & Row, 1963. P (Torchbook).

"The editors are aware that no American today can read a Puritan work without having a definite opinion of the author, and they in their turn have not been reticent in the introductory portions about speaking their minds; yet the larger purpose has been to supply enough of the Puritan literature itself to let each reader judge for himself." See next entry.

304. Miller, Perry. *The American Puritans: Their Prose and Poetry.* Garden City, N.Y.: Doubleday, 1956. P (Anchor Book).

A reduced version of the preceding anthology: "A few

items not in that volume are added, and I have tried to retain those that have proved of general interest."

305. Miller, Perry. *The Transcendentalists*. Cambridge, Mass.: Harvard University Press, 1950. P.

An anthology of the articles, essays, poems, and addresses of the chief proponents of transcendentalism in New England. See next entry.

306. Miller, Perry. *The American Transcendentalists: Their Prose and Poetry*. Garden City, N.Y.: Doubleday, 1957. P (Anchor Book).

"This volume is an offshoot of a more comprehensive anthology, *The Transcendentalists*. . . . This may be called an off-center collection of the material, designed to illustrate its range, to exemplify the variety, to set forth the general frame of mind and temper."

307. Miller, Perry. *American Thought: Civil War to World War I*. New York: Holt, Rinehart and Winston, 1954. P.

An anthology of selections from Josiah Royce, Chauncey Wright, Henry George, William Graham Sumner, C. S. Peirce, William James, John Dewey, and others.

308. Monroe, Harriet, and Alice Corbin Henderson. *The New Poetry: An Anthology of Twentieth-Century Verse in English*. New York: Macmillan, 1917. Enl. ed., 1923.

"During the last three or four years [i.e., from 1912 to 1916] there has been a remarkable renascence of poetry in both America and England, and an equally extraordinary revival of public interest in the art. The editors of this anthology wish to present in convenient form representative work of the poets who are today creating what is commonly called 'the new poetry' [including H. D., Frost, Vachel Lindsay, Amy Lowell, Edgar Lee Masters, Pound, Robinson, Sandburg, Stevens, and W. C. Williams]. Many critics feel that poetry is coming nearer than either the novel or the drama to the actual life of our time. The magazine *Poetry*, ever since its foundation in October, 1912, has encouraged this new spirit in the art, and the anthology is a further effort on the part of its editors to present the new spirit to the public.

"What is the new poetry? and wherein does it differ from the old? The difference is not in mere details of form, for much poetry infused with the new spirit conforms to the old measures and rhyme-schemes. It is not merely in diction, though the truly modern poet rejects the so-called 'poetic' shifts of language—the _deems, 'neaths, forsooths_, etc., the inversions of high-sounding rotundities, familiar to his predecessors: all the rhetorical excesses through which most Victorian poetry now seems 'over-appareled'. . . . The new poetry strives for a concrete and immediate realization of life; it would discard the theory, the abstraction, the remoteness, found in all classics not of the first order. It is less vague, less verbose, less eloquent, than most poetry of the Victorian period and much work of earlier periods. It has set before itself an ideal of absolute simplicity and sincerity—an ideal which implies an individual, unstereotyped diction; and an individual, unstereotyped rhythm. Thus inspired, it becomes intensive rather than diffuse. It looks out more eagerly than in; it becomes objective. The term 'exteriority' has been applied to it, but this is incomplete. In presenting the concrete object or the concrete environment, whether these be beautiful or ugly, it seeks to give more precisely the emotion arising from them, and thus widens immeasurably the scope of the art."

309.   Nevins, Allan. _America through British Eyes_. New York: Oxford University Press, 1948. Rev. and enl. ed. of _American Social History as Recorded by British Travellers_, published in 1923.

A carefully edited collection of British travel writings. "However well known certain conspicuous titles are [such as Frances Trollope's _Domestic Manners of the Americans_ and Dickens' _American Notes_], the great body of this travel literature is unexplored by ordinary American readers—and, indeed, is largely inaccessible. Relatively few of the books are kept in print, and not many are to be found outside the largest libraries. For these reasons a real place exists for a volume that furnishes characteristic and interesting passages from several scores of the most illuminating works, and which summarizes the contents of a good many more." Includes an extensive annotated bibliography.

The tables are turned at last in a recent book edited by Henry Steele Commager—_Britain through American Eyes_ (New York: McGraw-Hill, 1974).

310.   Nye, Russel B., and Norman S. Grabo. _American Thought and Writing_. 2 vols.: _The Colonial Period_ and _The Revolution and the_

Early Republic. Boston: Houghton Mifflin, 1965. P (Riverside Edition).

While these volumes contain some of the works conventionally included in anthologies of American literature, they range beyond such anthologies by presenting many lesser known literary figures as well as writers whose works trace the historical, intellectual, and cultural climate in America, from John Smith's *True Relation of ... Virginia* (1608) to William Dunlap's *André* (1798).

311.   *The Oxford Book of American Verse*. Ed. Bliss Carman. New York: Oxford University Press, 1927. 2nd ed., ed. F. O. Matthiessen, New York: Oxford University Press, 1950.

Carman provides a short introduction on the difficulties of compiling such a volume and makes selections which tend to emphasize the more popular work of poets such as Whittier, Longfellow, and Holmes. Matthiessen, who gives a much longer critical introduction on the development of American poetry, explicitly rejects Carman's method and provides selections which lead up to and away from the pivotal figure of Walt Whitman. Both editions are arranged chronologically, without notes.

312.   Pizer, Donald. *American Thought and Writing: The 1890's*. Boston: Houghton Mifflin, 1972. P.

"Most writers about the period are substantially in agreement with Harold Faulkner's belief [expressed in *Politics, Reform, and Expansion, 1890-1900*] that the 1890's were distinguished less by major social changes than by a full realization of changes which had already occurred—in particular, the change from a predominantly rural, agrarian civilization to an urban, industrial society. The problem presented by this realization was that many of the values and beliefs nurtured by the old ways of life seemed obsolete or inapplicable within the new.... The present book ... consists almost entirely of material selected from the works of writers of the decade" organized in nine sections on belief, literary criticism, the woman question, the West as theme and symbol, the city, the social crisis, varieties of escape, the war as catalyst, and the sense of the tragic.

313.   Sanders, G. D., J. H. Nelson, and M. L. Rosenthal. *Chief Modern Poets of Britain and America*. 5th ed. New York: Macmillan, 1970. P (2 vols.). This useful collection is divided into two volumes in the paperbound edition: *Poets of Britain* and *Poets of America*.

314. Silverman, Kenneth. *Colonial American Poetry*. New York: Hafner, 1968.

"More often than not, my choice of poems has been guided by the question, What did the settlers who cared enough to write about it think about America?"

315. Stegner, Wallace. *Selected American Prose, 1841-1900: The Realistic Movement*. New York: Holt, Rinehart and Winston, 1958. P.

A useful collection, perceptively introduced, organized in four sections: "The Native Roots of Realism: Travel and Humor"; "Local Color"; "Soldiers and Civilians"; and "The Winds of Doctrine: Defining Realism."

316. Taylor, J. Golden. *The Literature of the American West*. Boston: Houghton Mifflin, 1971. P.

"I have planned this anthology [which is organized according to genre] as a basic textbook for the course, Western American Literature, which is now taught in most of the colleges and universities this side of the Missouri River [Taylor was writing in Fort Collins, Colorado]. There is some evidence that it can also serve well as a supplementary text for the American Literature Survey—since the thirty-seven single- and multiple-volume anthologies on my shelves purporting to survey American literature with few exceptions attest to a certain literary innocence about the West."

317. Trachtenberg, Alan, et al. *The City: American Experience*. New York: Oxford University Press, 1971. P.

"Most readers will expect that a book on the experience of the city will deal with such specific issues as politics, economics, family structure, mental health, transportation— issues which affect the majority of the population. This collection [of sixty stories, essays, and poems and seventy-two photographs] has a different intent. It does not mean to address itself to concrete urban problems, at least not directly. We do not deal with explicit social patterns or with statistics. Our aim is to assemble materials which compose a city of the mind, of feelings and imagination, a composite city rendered from the experience of America's city people: European immigrant, black migrant, ghetto dweller, student, intellectual, worker, poet, historian, social critic, visionary planner."

318. Turner, Darwin T. *Black American Literature*. 3 vols. Columbus, Ohio: Merrill, 1969. P.

These short volumes—about 150 pages each—of fiction, poetry, and essays attempt "to provide a reasonably representative picture of the literary achievements throughout the twentieth century," with some attention to nineteenth-century writers. "If it seems that too much space has been given to the early writers, the reason is my belief that, because works of the past decade are available in libraries and paper-backed books, it is important in an anthology to provide readers with selections which may be more difficult to obtain."

319. Turner, Frederick W. *The Portable North American Indian Reader*. New York: Viking, 1974. P.

An excellent collection of "the remains of the past and the realities of the present" divided into "Myths and Tales" ("a historical and referential base for all that follows"), "Poetry and Oratory," "Culture Contact" ("these white voices speak as if they were describing a cultural and historical vacuum, as if nothing in America had actuality before their own intrusions"), "Image and Anti-Image" ("we begin here with the conflicting popular images of the Indian in white literature and subliterature, pass to contemporary re-evaluations of these old images, but end up in the hands of the subject himself").

"If you think about it for a moment, it will appear odd that after more than four centuries on this continent it should seem necessary to introduce anyone to what must have been the first and most engaging fact of the New World itself: the people who lived here. And yet, to judge from the evidence of American history past and present, this is precisely our need. . . . The great lesson which the history of the American Indian has for us [is] the knowledge *and* the acceptance of what it is to be human in a world with many forms of life. . . . In the gap between our own culturally conditioned view of the world and that of another with a radically different orientation . . . we may catch a glimpse of the way the world really is."

Important earlier anthologies of Indian literature include George W. Cronyn's *American Indian Poetry: An Anthology of Songs and Chants* (1934; originally published as *The Path on the Rainbow* in 1918 after many of the selections had appeared in

Poetry and other magazines); Margot Astrov's *The Winged Serpent: An Anthology of American Indian Prose and Poetry* (1946; includes South American Indian literature); and Jerome Rothenberg's *Shaking the Pumpkin: Traditional Poetry of the Indian North Americas* (1972).

320. Warfel, Harry R., and G. Harrison Orians. *American Local-Color Stories.* New York: American Book Co., 1941.

Contains sixty-three stories by thirty-eight local colorists, a substantial introduction, and an appendix listing writers and works by regions.

321. Wilson, Edmund. *The Shock of Recognition: The Development of Literature in the United States Recorded by the Men Who Made It.* 2 vols. 1943. Rpt. New York: Grosset & Dunlap, 1955.

Not an anthology of essays by professional literary critics, this collection reprints articles by American authors in order "to show the effect on one another of the first-rate American figures." Includes Howells' *My Mark Twain* and Henry James's *Hawthorne*; and—an exception to the general principle of organization—D. H. Lawrence's *Studies in Classic American Literature*.

VI Journals

330. *Abstracts of English Studies.* 1958—. $7.00.

Founded in 1958 (with bibliographical coverage for 1957), *AES* is an official publication of the National Council of Teachers of English, issued at the University of Colorado, Boulder, ten times a year on a monthly basis from September through June. "Approximately 1,100 journals are screened for articles dealing with American, English, and British Commonwealth literature and English language.... *AES* abstracts ... state the thesis, express the method of development, and point to the major implications drawn by the articles." Provides both monthly and annual indexes of names, titles, and subjects.

331. *American Literary Realism, 1870-1910.* 1967—. $5.00.

A "literary journal with a bibliographic focus ... intended to serve as a primary research tool in the area of American Literary Realism" which places special emphasis on the "lesser literary figures." Bibliographies of writings, bibliographies of secondary comment, and bibliographical essays on the following authors have appeared through Vol. 7 (1974): Adams, Ade, Alcott, J. L. Allen, M. H. Austin, Bierce, S. Bonner, A. Brown, C. F. Browne, Cahan, Chesnutt, Chopin, F. M. Crawford, Richard H. Davis, De Forest, Dreiser, M. H. Foote, Frederic, Freeman, Fuller, Gale, Garland, Glaspell, J. C. Harris, Harte, Hay, Howe, Howells (Special Supplement, 1969), H. H. Jackson, Jewett, Kirkland, Locke, London, H. M. Lyon, S. W. Mitchell, Moody, Murfree, Phillips, R. E. Robinson, Stowe, Whitlock, Wister, Woolson. See the cumulative index to each Autumn issue. Published quarterly by the Department of English at the University of Texas at Arlington.

332. *American Literature: A Journal of Literary History, Criticism, and Bibliography.* 1929—. $8.00 (half-price subscriptions available to students).

The leading journal in the field, *AL* concentrates specifically on "American authors and their works, past and present." It is published quarterly with the cooperation of the American Literature Section of the Modern Language Association by the Duke University Press. *AL* lists "Articles on American Literature Appearing in Current Periodicals" and "Research in Progress" in each issue. See **42** for Thomas Marshall's *Analytical Index to* American Literature.

333. *American Quarterly.* 1949—. $15.00 ($7.50 for students).

Published five times a year by the University of Pennsylvania in cooperation with the American Studies Association, *AQ* aims to "aid in giving a sense of direction to studies in the culture of the United States, past and present." Since 1955 the annual Summer Supplement has contained a selective, annotated list of "Articles in American Studies," a "unique annotated bibliography of interdisciplinary periodical articles dealing with the characteristics, relationships and ramifications of various aspects of American Civilization." See **15** for Hennig Cohen's two-volume compilation of these annual bibliographies. The Midcontinent American Studies Association also publishes a semiannual journal, *American Studies,* in cooperation with the University of Kansas.

334. *American Speech: A Quarterly of Linguistic Usage.* 1925—. $6.00.

Founded by Louise Pound under the sponsorship of the American Dialect Society, this journal contains "articles dealing with current usage, dialectology, and the history and structure of English." Emphasis is on English in the Western Hemisphere, "although contributions dealing with English in other parts of the world, with other languages influencing English or influenced by it, and with general linguistic theory may also be submitted for consideration by the editorial board."

335. *Contemporary Literature.* 1960—. $10.00.

Founded as *Wisconsin Studies in Contemporary Literature* (retitled in 1967), *CL*, published by the University of Wisconsin Press, is a critical quarterly "primarily devoted to a consideration of the new literature which has emerged since World War II, on both sides of the Atlantic." Special attention is paid to

"younger authors . . . viewed against the backgrounds of the
major concerns which inform contemporary writing." Special
issues, published irregularly, focus on individual topics, such
as "Existentialism in the 50's" (1960) and "The Objectivist
Poets" (1968); and authors, such as Salinger (1963), Nabokov
(1967), and H[ilda] D[oolittle] (1969). Occasional bibliographies.

336. *Early American Literature*. 1966—. $5.00.

Entitled *Early American Literature Newsletter* during 1966-67,
EAL is published three times yearly with the cooperation of
the MLA Early American Literature Group by the University
of Massachusetts. Includes studies of American literature of
the seventeenth and eighteenth centuries. Occasional bibliographic issues.

337. *Journal of American Folklore*. 1888—. $10.00 ($5.00, for students); $5.00 for *Abstracts*.

The official publication of the American Folklore Society,
JAF was published through a series of independent publishing houses until 1966, when it was taken over by the University of Texas Press. A quarterly which covers a wide range of
topics (from "African Backgrounds for American Negro
Folktales" to "The Folklore of the Heroin Addict"), it prints
both book and record reviews, occasionally devotes special
numbers to specific topics, and sponsors a separate quarterly,
Abstracts of Folklore Studies.

338. Journal of American Studies. 1967—. 40s. U.K. (U.S.A.
$9.00).

Published twice a year in London by the Cambridge University Press for the British Association for American Studies,
JAS was founded "to promote the study of the history, institutions, literature and culture of the United States. It publishes
work by specialists of any nationality on American history,
literature, politics, geography and related subjects. Articles
which cross the conventional lines of those disciplines are
welcome, as are comparative studies of American and other
cultures."

339. *Journal of Modern Literature*. 1970. $8.00.

Published five times yearly by Temple University. Since
March 1971 *JML* has published a yearly summary (entitled
Annual Record) of "scholarly activity on the modernist

period—book reviews, annotated bibliography, dissertations
completed, research in progress, news of conferences and
graduate programs, and other information."

340. *Journal of Popular Culture.* 1967—. $15.00 ($7.50 for students).

The official publication of the Popular Literature Section
of the Modern Language Association, the *Journal* is a quarterly "dedicated to 'Popular Culture' in the broadest sense of
the term." Articles have ranged from "The Theatre of Graffiti" and "Long Hair" to "The Morphology of the English
Metrical Romance." It includes film and record reviews. Published at Bowling Green University.

342. *The Mississippi Quarterly: The Journal of Southern Culture.*
1947—. $6.00 ($3.00 for students).

An interdisciplinary journal dealing with all aspects of the
life and civilization of the American South sponsored by
Mississippi State University. The summer issue has been devoted to Faulkner studies since 1964. Since 1969 the spring
issue has contained an annual annotated bibliography of
scholarship on Southern literature prepared by the Society
for the Study of Southern Literature.

343. *Modern Drama.* 1958—. $6.00.

A quarterly, founded, at the University of Kansas, which
contains articles and book reviews on drama since Ibsen, with
some emphasis on non-American scholarship. The September issue includes a selective bibliography organized by
country and author.

344. *Modern Fiction Studies.* 1955—. $6.00.

A critical quarterly founded by the Purdue University Department of English to promote the study of the "criticism,
scholarship, and bibliography of American, English, and
European fiction since about 1880." Two issues a year are
special numbers dealing with individual authors and containing bibliographies. These have included Stephen Crane (Fall
1959), Faulkner (Autumn 1956; Spring 1967), Fitzgerald
(Spring 1961), Hemingway (Autumn 1955; Autumn 1968),
Howells (Autumn 1970), Henry James (Spring 1957; Spring
1966), Melville (Fall 1962), Salinger (Autumn 1966), Steinbeck (Spring 1965), Mark Twain (Spring 1968), Robert Penn
Warren (Spring 1960), and Thomas Wolfe (Spring 1956;
Autumn 1965).

345. *New England Quarterly.* 1928—. $8.00.

"An historical review of New England life and letters," which publishes articles, notes, and book reviews on the history, literature, and general culture of the region.

346. *PMLA: Publications of the Modern Language Association of America.* 1884—.

The Modern Language Association is the trade union for many of those who toil in literary fields. Formed in 1883 as an innovative counter to the then prevailing notions of classical education, the MLA has expanded over the years (there are approximately 30,000 members) and surrounded itself with a formidable bureaucracy. Recent meetings have been enlivened by debates concerning the representation of minority groups and women in the profession, the political responsibilities of scholars, and whether the MLA itself is an enlightened force for intellectual leadership or a regressive arm of the military-industrial-educational complex. Annual dues are $25.00 to $35.00, depending on salary ($10.00 for student membership), and include a subscription to the six issues of *PMLA* and one volume each from the separate, annually published, multivolume *MLA International Bibliography* and *MLA Abstracts* (**45**). The September (Directory) issue of *PMLA* contains useful lists of members and department chairmen. The MLA also publishes a newsletter, holds an annual convention in late December, and runs a job information service (which includes the publication of *Job Information Lists* in October, December, February and May).

Commencing January 1975, *PMLA* "will no longer serve simply as another 'general' periodical in which members may publish their findings, no matter how specialized or esoteric, but will instead attempt to provide a single source through which members of the profession can be informed of the most *significant* developments in scholarship and criticism in all areas of modern language and literature.

"The editorial policy . . . stipulates that *PMLA* articles must be 'of significant interest to the entire membership of the Association,' and must normally (1) employ a widely applicable approach or methodology; or (2) use an interdisciplinary approach of importance to the interpretation of literature; or (3) treat a broad subject or theme; or (4) treat a major author or work; or (5) discuss a minor author or work in such a way as to bring insight to a major author, work, genre, period, or critical method."

Members of MLA interested in American literature may also want to join the separate American Literature Section of the Modern Language Association (MLA membership does not confer membership in the Section). Dues are $4.00 per year, payable to

William Mulder, Sec'y.-Treas., ALS
Spencer Hall 341-D, University of Utah
Salt Lake City, Utah 84102

"The American Literature Section is a national and international group devoted to the furthering of ideals of American literary scholarship through research, association, publications, special committees on bibliographies and manuscript holdings and archives, and through the reading of papers at the annual MLA meetings. The Section elects the members of the Editorial Board of *American Literature* and (through its member-elected Advisory Council) the members of the Advisory Committee of the Center on Editions of American Authors. The Section also sponsors the award of the Hubbell medalion to distinguished scholars. General meetings of the Section are held annually as well as the meetings of the various sub-groups of the Section:

Group 1, Seventeenth and Eighteenth Century
Group 2, Early Nineteenth Century
Group 3, Late Nineteenth Century
Group 4, Twentieth Century

Membership in the Section is open only to members of the MLA. Members of the Section receive each year the Annual Report (February) containing committee reports and abstracts of papers read at MLA meetings; a mail ballot (November) for the election of officers; and [a free copy of] *American Literary Scholarship* [5]."

347. *Proof: The Yearbook of American Bibliographical and Textual Studies.* 1971—. $20.00.

A clothbound annual founded in 1971 at the University of South Carolina.

348. *Resources for American Literary Study.* 1971—. $8.00.

"A new [Spring 1971] semi-annual journal devoted to the collection and dissemination of information about the resources for scholarship in American Literature" which plans to include "annotated and evaluative checklists of critical and biographical scholarship" on the works of major and minor authors in all periods of American literature as well as "evaluative bibliographical essays on major authors, works, genres, trends, and periods." Jointly sponsored by Virginia Commonwealth University and the University of Maryland.

349. *Studies in American Humor*. 1974—. $5.00 ($3.00 for students).

A new journal published by the Department of English at Southwest Texas State University. *SAH* divides the field with another new publication, *American Humor: An Interdisciplinary Newsletter*, issued jointly by the University of Maryland and Virginia Commonwealth University. *SAH* concentrates on literary humor, while *AH:IN* is more theoretical, interdisciplinary, and miscellaneous—devoted to "the study of American humor from a variety of perspectives including literature, popular culture, the comics, films, television, the stage."

350. *Studies in the Novel*. 1968—. $4.00.

Published quarterly at North Texas State University, Denton, Texas. Includes special numbers devoted to individual writers or related writers: Vol. I, No. 4 (Winter 1969)—Melville; Vol. II, No. 4 (Winter 1970)—Hawthorne; Vol. III, No. 2 (Summer 1971)—American Negro Novelists.

351. *Twentieth Century Literature: A Scholarly and Critical Journal*. 1955—. $6.00.

A quarterly journal founded by Alan Swallow (currently published by the Immaculate Heart College Press, Los Angeles), which prints "articles on all aspects of modern and contemporary literature, including articles in English on writers in other languages." Each number prints a selective "Current Bibliography," and there are occasional checklists published on major figures. See Pownall's *Articles on Twentieth Century Literature* (**50**) for a collection of the "Current Bibliography" sections from 1955 to 1970.

352. *Western American Literature*. 1967—. $7.00.

WAL is the quarterly journal of the Western Literature Association. The Winter issue includes a listing of theses and dissertations—completed and in progress—in the field. Published by Utah State University at Logan.

There are, in addition, a number of journals and newsletters devoted to individual (and grouped) American authors. These include:

353. *American Transcendental Quarterly.*

354. *Stephen Crane Newsletter.*

355. *Emily Dickinson Bulletin.*

356. *Dreiser Newsletter* (published semiannually since 1970).

357. *ESQ: A Journal of the American Renaissance* (founded in 1955 as the *Emerson Society Quarterly*).

358. *Fitzgerald/Hemingway Annual* (hardbound annual since 1969, which supplanted the *Fitzgerald Newsletter*, 1958-68).

359. *Frederic Herald.*

360. *Hawthorne Journal* (hardbound annual since 1971).

361. *Sinclair Lewis Newsletter.*

362. *Jack London Newsletter.*

363. *Lost Generation Journal* (commenced May 1973).

364. *Markham Review* (publishes short articles on "the American literary scene of the period 1865-1940").

365. *Poe Studies* (formerly *Poe Newsletter*).

366. *Steinbeck Quarterly.*

367. *Studies in the American Renaissance* (projected to begin in the

368. *Thoreau Journal Quarterly.*

369. *Thoreau Society Bulletin.*

370. *Thoth* (includes Stephen Crane bibliography annually in the Spring number).

371. *Mark Twain Journal* (formerly *Mark Twain Quarterly*).

372. *Twainian.*

373. *Walt Whitman Review* (formerly *Walt Whitman Newsletter*).

Note: A list of journals publishing articles on American literature may be found in the March issue of *American Literature* (**332**); an exhaustive "Master List" is published in each issue of the *MLA International Bibliography* (**45**).

Author, Subject, and Genre Index

Author, Subject, and Genre Index

This index is a single alphabetical list of authors, editors, and compilers of secondary works (regular type); selected subjects and genres (capitals); and American authors (capitals). The author entries refer the reader primarily to *Eight American Authors* (**66**), *Fifteen American Authors before 1900* (**51**), *Sixteen Modern American Authors* (**12**), the Goldentree bibliography series (**13, 18, 32, 40, 47, 62**), and *American Literary Scholarship* (**5**), as well as special issues of journals devoted to individual authors. Additional information for these authors and information concerning authors not listed here can be found in *Literary History of the United States: Bibliography* (**58**) and the other bibliographies cited in Section I.

Numbers refer to entries, not pages.

anthologies, 294, 296, 308, 313
bibliography of criticism, 50
black poets, 272
criticism, 91, 181, 196, 200, 260
Southern literary renaissance, 86
survey of research and criticism on
    major authors, 12
twenties, 100, 101, 102, 123
Poirier, Richard (1925—), 175
POPULAR LITERATURE, 117, 160,
165, 340
reprints of popular novels, 270
Porte, Joel (1933—), 176
PORTER,   KATHERINE   ANNE
(1890—)
bibliography of criticism, 47
POUND, EZRA (1885-1972), 272
survey of research of criticism, 12
Pound, Louise (1872-1958), 334
Pownall, David E. (1925—), 50
PRESCOTT, WILLIAM HICKLING
(1796-1859), 278
bibliography of criticism, 13
PRINTING IN AMERICA, 60
PROGRESSIVE ERA, 260
PURDY, JAMES (1923—), 118
PYNCHON, THOMAS (1937—), 135,
166

Quinn, Arthur Hobson (1875-1960),
177, 178

RADICAL NOVEL, 120, 180
Rahv, Philip (1908—), 179
RANSOM, JOHN CROWE (1888-
1974), 58, 186
REALISM, 80, 90, 167, 174, 295, 315,
331
Rees, Robert A. (1935—), 51
REGIONAL LITERATURE
historical bibliography, 26
see also LOCAL COLOR
RELIGIOUS HISTORY OF AMERI-
CA, 76, 262
bibliography, 48
REPRINTS, 234
first edition facsimile reprints, 255,
258
REVIEWS
book reviews

digest of reviews, 7
review index, 8, 33, 42, 44
drama reviews, 1, 9, 16, 49, 55
fiction reviews (1870-1910), 21
reviews published during author's
    lifetime, 273
see also Section VI (Journals), esp.
    331-33, 335, 336, 342-45, 348
REVOLUTIONARY PERIOD, 205, 262
see also EARLY AMERICAN LIT-
ERATURE
RICE, ELMER (1892-1967)
bibliography of criticism, 40
Rideout, Walter B. (1917—), 180, 285
Robbins, J. Albert (1914—), 5
ROBERTS, ELIZABETH MADOX
(1886-1941)
bibliography of criticism, 47
ROBINSON, EDWIN ARLINGTON
(1869-1935), 272
bibliography of criticism, 13
survey of research and criticism, 12
Robinson, James K. (1916—), 285
ROBINSON, ROWLAND E. (1833-
1900)
bibliography of criticism, 331
ROETHKE, THEODORE (1908-63),
130, 182, 294
ROMANTICISM, 94, 110, 121, 143,
148, 167, 176
Rosenthal, M. L. (1917—), 181, 182, 313
ROTH, HENRY (1906—), 2
ROTH, PHILIP (1933—)
bibliography of criticism, 47
Rourke, Constance (1885-1941), 183,
184
Rubin, Louis D., Jr. (1923—), 52, 185,
186
RUKEYSER, MURIEL (1913—), 294
Ryan, Pat M. (1928—), 53

Sabin, Joseph (1821-81), 54
Salem, James M. (1937—), 55
SALINGER, J. D. (1919—)
bibliography of criticism, 47, 344
criticism, 335
SANDBURG, CARL (1878-1967), 181
Sanders, G. D. (1895—), 313
SANTAYANA, GEORGE (1863-1952)
bibliography of criticism, 13

TECHNOLOGY, 149, 199, 292
TEXTS OF AMERICAN AUTHORS,
255, 258, 266
critical editions, 267, 278
TEXTUAL STUDIES, 60, 347
THEATER, *see* DRAMA
THEORY OF CRITICISM, *see* CRITI-
CISM
THIRTIES (1930s), 130
THOREAU, HENRY DAVID (1817-62)
bibliography of criticism, 13
criticism, 150, 272
survey of research and criticism, 5, 66
Thorp, Willard (1899—), 200
THURBER, JAMES (1894-1961), 272
Thurston, Jarvis (1914—), 61
TIMROD, HENRY (1828-67)
bibliography of criticism, 13
TOCQUEVILLE, ALEXIS DE (1805-
59), 201
TOOMER, JEAN (1894-1967)
bibliography of criticism, 62
TOURGÉE, ALBION W. (1838-1905)
bibliography of criticism, 32, 58
Trachtenberg, Alan (1932—), 317
TRANSCENDENTALISM, 150, 305,
306
survey of research and criticism, 5
TRAVEL LITERATURE, 48
Trent, William P. (1862-1932), 92
Trilling, Lionel (1905—), 202
TRUMBULL, JOHN (1750-1831)
bibliography of criticism, 18
criticism, 129
TUCKER, GEORGE (1775-1861)
bibliography of criticism, 18
Turner, Darwin T. (1931—), 62, 318
Turner, Frederick W. (1937—), 319
Turpie, Mary C. (1909—), 139
Tuttleton, James W. (1934—), 203
TWAIN, MARK, *see* CLEMENS,
SAMUEL LANGHORNE
TWENTIES (1920s), 100, 101, 102, 123
TWENTIETH-CENTURY LITERA-
TURE
anthology, 293
bibliography, 35
bibliography of criticism, 50
criticism, 193, 196, 200, 213
journal, 351

see also DRAMA, NOVEL, POETRY
Tyler, Gary R., 16
Tyler, Moses Coit (1835-1900), 204, 205
TYLER, ROYALL (1757-1826)
bibliography of criticism, 18, 40

UPDIKE, JOHN (1932—)
bibliography of criticism, 47
USAGE, *see* DICTIONARIES OF
AMERICAN USAGE

Van den Bark, Melvin (1897-1974), 225
Van Doren, Carl (1885-1950), 206
VEBLEN, THORSTEIN (1857-1929),
278
VERNACULAR
vernacular tradition in the arts, 137
see also COLLOQUIAL SPEECH
VIDAL, GORE (1925—), 77
Vinson, James (1921—), 229
VONNEGUT, KURT, JR. (1922—),
135, 166

Waggoner, Hyatt W. (1913—), 207
WAGONER, DAVID (1926—), 130
Walcutt, Charles Child (1908—), 208
WALKER, DAVID (1785-1830), 79
Walker, Warren S. (1921—), 63
Ward, John William (1922—), 209
Warfel, Harry R. (1899-1971), 320
WARREN, ROBERT PENN (1905—)
bibliography of criticism, 47, 58, 344
WEBSTER, DANIEL (1782-1852)
bibliography of criticism, 18
WEBSTER, NOAH (1758-1843)
bibliography of criticism, 18
Wecter, Dixon (1906-50), 194
Wegelin, Christof (1911—), 210
WEISS, THEODORE (1916—), 130
WELTY, EUDORA (1909—)
bibliography of criticism, 47
Wentworth, Harold (1904—), 243
Wertheim, Stanley (1930—), 27
WESCOTT, GLENWAY (1901—)
bibliography of criticism, 47
WEST, NATHANAEL (NATHAN
WALLENSTEIN WEINSTEIN;
1902-40), 272
bibliography of criticism, 47
Westbrook, Max (1927—), 211